STANDARD LOAN

UNLESS RECALLED BY ANOTHER READER
THIS ITEM MAY BE BORROWED FOR

FOUR WEEKS

To renew, telephone:
01243 816089 (Bishop Otter)
01243 812099 (Bognor Regis)

ORSON
WELLES

FOREWORD BY
FRANÇOIS TRUFFAUT
Profile by Jean Cocteau

Translated from the French by
Jonathan Rosenbaum

ORSON WELLES

A Critical View

ANDRÉ BAZIN

Elm Tree Books · London

First published in Great Britain 1978 by Elm Tree Books/Hamish Hamilton Ltd. 90 Great
Russell Street, London WC1B 3 PT

Designed by Gloria Adelson

British Library Cataloguing in Publication Data

Bazin, André
  Orson Welles.
  1. Welles, Orson
  791.43'0233'0924   PN2287.W456
ISBN 0-241-89879-X

Printed in the United States of America

Contents

Foreword

—⚬—

by François Truffaut

—⚬—

André Bazin was a young critic at the time of the Paris opening of
Citizen Kane in July 1946. He was twenty-eight and had been a
professional critic for two years. Along with Marcel Carné's *Le Jour
Se Lève,* Jean Renoir's *La Règle du Jeu* and Charlie Chaplin's *Mon-
sieur Verdoux, Citizen Kane* is undoubtedly the film that excited him
the most.

Bazin's articles on Charlie Chaplin and Orson Welles made him
the leader of the young postwar critics who wrote for *L'Écran
Français* as well as *La Revue du Cinéma,* which expired after twenty
issues and was reborn as *Les Cahiers du Cinéma.*

Bazin's admiration for "the wonder kid from Kenosha," as
magazines were already styling him, was to remain undiminished,
for he devoted his first book, in 1950, to Welles, who had just shot
Macbeth and was preparing *Othello.* This little volume, superbly
prefaced by Jean Cocteau, quickly went out of print and became
a collector's item; and in 1958, shortly before his death, sparked
by enthusiasm for *Touch of Evil,* Bazin prepared a revised and

expanded edition, published here in Jonathan Rosenbaum's translation.

Over Christmas 1973, one of the gifts that the people of Hollywood delighted in giving was a framed version of a "Peanuts" cartoon by Schulz, published in the *Los Angeles Times*. This is what the seven drawings showed:

1. Linus turns on a television.
2. Lucy, his big sister, arrives and asks him: "What are you watching?"
3. Linus: *"Citizen Kane."*
4. Lucy: "I've seen it about ten times."
5. Linus: "This is the first time I've ever seen it. . . ."
6. Leaving the room, Lucy blurts out: " 'Rosebud' was his sled!"
7. Linus writhes in agony: "Aaugh!"

This "Peanuts" strip demonstrates, if any demonstration is needed, the cinematic and extracinematic position that *Citizen Kane* has assumed in the cultural life of two generations. Just as the silent cinema was modified and stimulated by Griffith's *The Birth of a Nation*, Stroheim's *Foolish Wives,* and Chaplin's three-reelers, everything that matters in cinema since 1940 has been influenced by *Citizen Kane* and Jean Renoir's *La Règle du Jeu.*

In his first films, Charlie Chaplin played the character of the poorest and most humble man in the world. Simply in order to eat, he was compelled to steal food from a baby or a dog. Within a few years the success of Chaplin's films made him the most celebrated figure in the world, and naturally this gradually led him to abandon the character of the little tramp. Beginning with *The Great Dictator,* Chaplin assumed his celebrity completely; after having envisaged playing Christ, then Napoleon, he took on Adolf Hitler, who, André Bazin noted, "had dared to steal Charlie's mustache." Succeeding Hinkel-Hitler came Verdoux-Landru, the most famous lady-killer in the twentieth century (the germ of this film was supplied to Chaplin by Orson Welles), *A King in New York* (Chaplin versus McCarthy's America), and finally the diplomat Ogden Mears of *The Countess from Hong Kong,* a film whose autobiographical aspect has escaped many critics, who haven't read the accounts of Chaplin's trips around the world and who didn't think it necessary to make a mental substitution of Chaplin himself for Marlon Brando while watching the film.

Like Chaplin's, Orson Welles' work is autobiographical in a subterranean manner, and it also pivots around the major theme of artistic creation, the search for identity.

The great difference between these two men—and therefore between their works—is that Orson Welles has never known destitution, and further, that his celebrity preceded his entry into cinema, mainly because of the repercussions of the *Mercury Theatre on the Air* broadcast of October 30, 1938, devoted to the adaptation of H. G. Wells' *The War of the Worlds.* Accounts of this radio event and the panic that ensued have been given countless times and I won't linger over it, except to note that Orson Welles' position just before shooting *Citizen Kane* was unusual and paradoxical: instead of having to make himself known and recognized, Welles, who was then only twenty-five, found himself in the reverse position of having to uphold a reputation that was already immense. For all sorts of reasons that are easy to imagine, Orson Welles, working in New York in theatre and radio, was more celebrated than popular across America; his exploits aroused more curiosity than sympathy. From the time of his arrival in California, the world of Hollywood fostered a basic hostility toward him, which, over the years, has never changed. So Welles in 1939 must have felt that it was necessary to offer the public not only *a good film* but *the* film, one that would summarize forty years of cinema while taking the opposite course to everything that had been done, a film that would be at once a balance sheet and a platform, a declaration of war on traditional cinema and a declaration of love for the medium.

André Bazin was correct to state that *"Citizen Kane* and *Ambersons* could finally be a matter of childhood tragedy." For that is indeed

3

the case, and certainly it is clear that the emotions Welles experienced in his youth molded the plot of *Citizen Kane,* even if, as Pauline Kael asserts, its theme and central character had been furnished by the co-scriptwriter Herman J. Mankiewicz (who would himself be more or less represented in the film by the character of the dramatic critic, Kane's college friend Jedediah Leland, played by Joseph Cotten).

Orson Welles is at his best when he tells stories about families: The Hollywood cinema of the period, sentimental and boy-scoutish, wasn't stingy in this respect, but Orson's familial vision scarcely resembles Louis B. Mayer's. In Welles' work, fathers, sons, uncles and aunts are of the possessive sort and the principal characters nearly always suffer from emotional traumas. Before Welles, this terrain of the confusions of adolescence had hardly been explored by Hollywood films, whose two favorite dialogue expressions seemed to be "You're a good boy, sonny" and "Daddy, you're the best pop in the world."

Orson Welles would never become an entirely American filmmaker for the good reason that he wasn't an entirely American child. Like Henry James, he would benefit from a cosmopolitan culture and would pay for this privilege with the disadvantage of not being able to feel at home anywhere; an American in Europe, a European in America, he will always be, if not a man torn, at least a man divided.

As an adolescent, with his father or his mother, Orson Welles visited Europe, China and Jamaica. His mother died during one of these trips, when Orson was eight, the age of the young Charles Foster Kane when he is forcibly separated from his mother: "Isn't it with the sled, whose perhaps unconscious memory will haunt him until his death, that he violently strikes, at the very outset of his life, the banker who has come to tear him from his play in the snow and his mother's protection, come to snatch him from his childhood to make him into Kane the citizen?" (André Bazin)

At ten, Orson Welles made himself up in his room as King Lear, and it was in the role of an old man that he made his debut in *The Jew Süss* in Dublin in 1932. Several anecdotes on Welles' childhood have been furnished to biographers by Dr. Bernstein, a friend of his parents who taught him magic tricks as a child and gave him a puppet theatre—the Bernstein whom one will find under the same name, magnificently portrayed by Everett Sloane in *Citizen Kane*. When Thompson, the investigator, attempts to learn more about Kane just after his death, he says to Bernstein, "After all, you were with him from the beginning . . ." and Bernstein replies, "From *before* the beginning, young fellow. And now it's after the end."

It is interesting to note that it was his precociousness—legendary but firmly verified—that forced Orson Welles to make himself look old, to adopt a prematurely deep voice and perhaps even to draw himself false wrinkles; his parents took him along everywhere and let him participate in the adult conversations. In order to avoid being constantly made fun of, this youngster given to grown-up utterances found himself constrained *to play a role*, and one can thus suppose that necessity preceded the taste for acting and perhaps even created it.

In his book *The Fabulous Orson Welles,* Peter Noble cites a Wisconsin newspaper which devoted an article to the young Orson Welles: "Cartoonist, Actor, Poet—and only Ten!" I am inclined to mistrust anecdotes on Welles' childhood, for they all sound very journalistic and are copied while being expanded from one book to the next; and yet, if they are not all true, they are all believable in the light of what we know about the man today.

In 1934, for a daily NBC broadcast that attempted to tell the news while dramatizing it, Welles was induced to impersonate the voices of Hitler and Mussolini. It was this same *March of Time* broadcast that he would transform into a newsreel, by way of a prologue, in the first reel of *Citizen Kane*. The success of this broadcast led Welles to move from NBC to the rival network CBS, and one will find a possible transposition of this transfer in *Citizen Kane*, when the entire journalistic staff that it has taken the *Chronicle* twenty years to set up goes off to join Kane's *Inquirer*.

While we are concerned with the notion of a staff transfer, it is clear that since the Mercury Theatre group was formed in 1939 out of a dozen or so actors whom Orson Welles had brought together and admired, the initial casting of *Citizen Kane* preceded the construction of the screenplay and even strongly determined what gives the film a homogeneity indiscernible at that period in the productions of the major companies. "The Mercury group constituted a superb orchestra," declared Bernard Herrmann, who was the group's composer and wrote the scores of *Kane* and *Ambersons.* It was in 1935 that John Houseman offered Orson Welles the leading role in *Panic,* a verse play by Archibald MacLeish about the Wall Street collapse of 1929. Orson played the character of a powerful and dishonest banker. Shortly afterward he played an idealistic young Frenchman who opposed an assembly of armaments dealers in *Ten Million Ghosts,* whose staging, to judge from contemporary accounts, prefigured *Citizen Kane* (although it was not directed by Welles).

By this enumeration of autobiographical elements in *Citizen Kane,* I am not proposing to enter into polemics with Pauline Kael, according to whom Herman J. Mankiewicz was the sole author of *Citizen Kane*'s script. As she is herself a writer, I can understand her attempt to bring into the limelight a man who had indeed been forgotten in the affair—to the point where no European or American critic to my knowledge thought of mentioning *Citizen Kane* when Joseph L. Mankiewicz, Herman's brother, made *The Barefoot Contessa,* which charts the stages in the career of a Hollywood star while using a structure very close to *Citizen Kane*'s, including a big argument/separation scene repeated and relayed by two complementary witnesses two reels apart. Let us further note that the influence of *Kane* is detectable in a good number of films over the past thirty-five years, the best of these probably being Federico Fellini's *8½.*

It is worth noting that the considerable amount of visual and scripted material concocted in *Citizen Kane* would have amply justified a three-hour film (and I am one of those who attach more importance to *Citizen Kane* than to *Gone With the Wind!*). For *Kane* runs exactly one hour and fifty-nine minutes, and it isn't the least merit of Orson Welles to have placed three pints of liquid in a two-pint bottle. The whole problem for the film-maker—no, not the *whole* problem but a substantial part of it—is to learn how to come to grips with running time. In many films, the expositional scenes are too long, the "privileged" scenes too short, which winds up equalizing everything and leads to rhythmic monotony. Here again, we can say that Welles benefited from his experience as a radio storyteller, for he must have had to learn to differentiate sharply between expositional scenes (reduced to flashes of four to eight seconds) and genuine emotional scenes of three to four minutes.

In the usual Hollywood film, a screenplay is a literary object which reads like a play and only awaits the arrival of a director to become a film or, more precisely, what Hitchcock labels with justified contempt, "photographs of people talking." Here, in *Kane*, we have a film where the voices count as much as the words, dialogue which has characters speaking at the same time like musical instruments in a score, with sentences left unfinished as in life. This antitraditional procedure—scarcely imitated afterward, since it is difficult to master perfectly—culminates in the "love nest" scene, which counterposes the two actresses in the film, the wife and the mistress, along with the politician Jim Gettys and Kane himself.

Thanks to this quasi-musical conception of dialogue, *Citizen Kane* "breathes" differently from most films. Stemming from the Mankiewicz-Welles collaboration, the shooting script obviously doesn't constitute a literary work but is already a first *mise en scène.* The direction comprises a second *mise en scène,* the editing a third. It is very generous on Pauline Kael's part to erect a posthumous statue to Herman J. Mankiewicz; all the same, the screenplay of *Citizen Kane* is not in any way a script by a "scriptwriter" but *a script by a director.*

Pauline Kael reproaches Orson Welles for having assumed sole responsibility for authorship of the *Citizen Kane* script in some interview or another.* But in André Bazin's archives I have found an issue of the weekly *L'Écran Français* of September 21, 1948, containing the first interview with Welles by Bazin himself and Jean-Claude Tachella, today a film-maker. In the course of this first meeting, recorded at the Venice Festival, where Welles was presenting *Macbeth*, Welles declared to Bazin: "Four of us wrote the *Kane* script. Only Mankiewicz and I were credited, but it should be said that Joseph Cotten and John Houseman are also authors of *Citizen Kane.*"

Finally, again by Pauline Kael's account, Rosebud is the only element in the script whose paternity has been denied by Mankiewicz *and* Welles, each declaring that the other is responsible for it; it is a matter—Pauline Kael, Welles and Mankiewicz agree only on this point—of a rather cheap Freudian gimmick which would eventually seem like a blemish on the film. I must confess that I don't share this viewpoint: Rosebud seems to me as good as Ali Baba's "Open Sesame," and indeed, if someone spread the rumor that Truffaut had invented Rosebud, I would be honored by the attribution.

To seek to distinguish the influences which have given a work its definitive form is not to diminish its value. Just before beginning a film, a film-maker becomes so mobilized by his project that his awareness is sharpened in the process: everything that he sees, reads and hears furnishes him with material for reflection or creation. In Orson Welles' case, however, the spirit of contrariness is so strong that the influences show themselves more readily in an inverse fashion; that is, I suspect him of having watched other films

*The phrase quoted by Kael in French ("Le seul film que j'aie jamais écrit du premier au dernier mot et pu mener à bien est *Citizen Kane*") *comes from a cutting continuity of the film published in French (l'Avant-Scène du cinéma* No. 11, 15 January 1962, p. 27), but this in turn appears to derive from Bazin's first *extended* interview with Welles, which is quoted extensively in the last chapter of this book. The phrase in question occurs in the penultimate paragraph and is practically indentical: "Le seul film que j'ai écrit du premier au dernier mot et pu mener à bonne fin est *Citizen Kane* . . ." Considering the fact that the original English transcript of the interview is no longer available, and the the process of editing *and* translation in such interviews was often far from precise, it is at least open to question whether Welles in fact ever claimed sole authorship of the *Citizen Kane* script in the first place. (*Trans.*)

not to gain inspiration, but rather to take systematically the opposite course!

According to a legend that has persisted too long, Orson Welles saw no films before starting *Citizen Kane*. The first feet of film exposed under his direction, at Woodstock in 1934, have been rediscovered: *The Hearts of Ages,* a little film fragment four minutes long—shot over only a day or two—was shown to me in Los Angeles. As is often the case with a first film, what we see is a succession of shots filmed without any concern for linkage or continuity; all the creative effort is concentrated on the deliberately extreme makeup—Orson, age nineteen, acting with a false skull—and on plastic attitudes. It isn't an avant-garde film but a parody of the avant-garde (sexual symbols, an accumulation of macabre elements). It was Carl Dreyer whom I thought of most frequently, but Welles himself, questioned on French television about this film, explained that he had shot it to make fun of two avant-garde films that could be seen at the time only in specialized theatres: Luis Buñuel's *Un Chien Andalou* and Jean Cocteau's *Le Sang d'un Poète;* he added, with obvious sincerity, that he had since changed his mind and that today he greatly admired both film-makers.

This anecdote interests me because it illustrates a duality, a contradiction that persists today and means, for instance, that when a journalist tries to flatter Welles by denigrating Hollywood, Orson always refuses to play this demagogical game. This is where the duality lies: Orson Welles is a poet *in spite of himself.* He is a poet who would love to be a prose-writer (which explains his admiration for De Sica, Renoir, Joseph Conrad, Karen Blixen, Marcel Pagnol and John Ford). His conception of cinema being above all musical —as I've just had occasion to point out—he has been brought to make films that are different from what he likes in other films.*
Welles was certainly sincere in his hostility toward Cocteau, Buñuel and Eisenstein, for if he is, like them, a poet, he has another

*It is well established today that Welles has always been a film-lover, and one may recall here his list of the world's ten best films in *Sight and Sound,* July–September 1952: *City Lights, Intolerance, Shoeshine, The Baker's Wife, Stagecoach, Greed, Nanook of the North, Potemkim, La Grande Illusion, Our Daily Bread.*

9

conception of cinematic poetry. Having come to cinema not only from theatre but also from radio—a point that has long been overlooked—Orson Welles, unlike Eisenstein and Dreyer, has never considered film as a plastic object but rather as a duration, something which unwinds like a ribbon; he has defined film, in fact, as "a ribbon of dreams."

His radio experience taught him never to leave a film in repose, to set up aural bridges from one scene to the next, making use of music as no one had before him, to capture or stimulate awareness, to play with the volume of voices at least as much as the words. Which is why—independently of the great visual pleasures they afford us—Orson Welles' films also make marvelous radio broadcasts; I have verified this by recording all of them on cassettes, which I listen to in my bathroom with ever renewed delight.

To return to the question of influences: Orson Welles has never sought to conceal what he gained from seeing other films brought to him, particularly John Ford's *Stagecoach*, which he says somewhere he saw many times before shooting *Citizen Kane*.

In *Stagecoach*, John Ford systematically showed ceilings each time the characters left the stagecoach to enter a way station. I imagine that John Ford in fact filmed these ceilings to create a contrast with the long shots of the stagecoach's journey, where the sky inevitably occupied a large portion of the screen.

The use of ceilings in *Citizen Kane* is quite different, as André Bazin explains:

> The persistence of the low angle in *Citizen Kane* means . . . that we quickly cease to have a clear awareness of technique even while we continue to submit to its mastery. Thus it is much more likely that the method corresponds to a precise aesthetic intention: to impose a particular vision of drama on us. A vision that could be called infernal, since the gaze upward seems to come out of the earth while the ceilings, forbidding any escape within the décor, complete the fatality of this curse.

Bazin's explication of Welles' ceilings is persuasive and judicious; I would add, however, the following hypothesis: Orson Welles' favorite angle led him to place the camera on the ground, but doesn't that bring him by the same token to present his protagonists as we would see them in the theatre if we were seated in the first ten rows of the orchestra? Before Welles, all sorts of film directors shot movies not only without showing the ceilings of sets, but without even raising the question of whether there was any need to show them. Catapulted from theatre and radio into cinema, Orson Welles quite naturally began to ask himself about the differences and common points between the various media. The use of the low angle—which gives the viewpoint of the spectator in the orchestra or that of the theatre director conducting a rehearsal in the auditorium—necessarily entails the use of lenses with a short focal length (which yield a larger vision), for any other lens used at this angle would only eliminate depth and destroy the notion of space.

So in my opinion, Welles' thoughts as he embarked on the cinema could be summed up as follows: I'm going to make a film that will present all the advantages of radio and theatre without their disadvantages, with the result that my film will be unlike any other that has been made. Pride comes into this conception, but then as Godard says in *Contempt,* "One has to be proud when one is making films."

Before regretfully taking leave of *Citizen Kane,* I'd like to add that if anyone is tempted to recognize William Randolph Hearst or Howard Hughes behind the character of Charles Foster Kane, or Basil Zaharoff behind Gregory Arkadin, no one could—or should —care less. Returning to San Francisco by car, I was shown Hearst's San Simeon on the way with the suggestion that I visit it; I refused because it isn't San Simeon that interests me but Xanadu, not the reality but the work of art on film. Autobiographical sources are more interesting than biographies, but although they may explain the *why,* they don't explain the *how,* and in any case they miss what's important. As we all know, there are autobiographical film-makers whose work interests no one. The only way to speak about Orson Welles is to enumerate the beauties of his films, an exciting task that twenty volumes wouldn't exhaust. The excellent work of Roy Fowler, Peter Noble, Ronald Gottesman, Charles Higham, Peter Cowie, André Bazin, Maurice Bessy, Joseph McBride, Pauline Kael, Bob Thomas and Peter Bogdanovich forms a cluster of projectors which illuminate the artist from every side and track him down, like poor Tony Camonte, tormented behind the shuttered window of his hideaway at the end of *Scarface!*

After *Citizen Kane,* Orson Welles undertook *The Magnificent Ambersons* from a novel by Booth Tarkington. Contrary to what has sometimes been said, it is a marvelous novel. Reading it, one realizes that the adaptation by Welles—who felt that he had a close intimacy with the book, having already adapted it for his radio show—is pretty faithful to it, if one takes into account the work of tightening it up, necessary in adapting a story which extends over a long period. To my mind, Welles' best alteration resides in the elimination of the character of Fred Kinney, boyfriend of Eugene Morgan's daughter Lucy. Indeed, the rivalry in the novel between George Amberson Minafer and Fred Kinney detracts from the real clash established with much greater force between George (Tim Holt) and Eugene (Joseph Cotten), who wants to marry George's mother, a purely emotional conflict in which Isabel Amberson Minafer (Dolores Costello) is the Jocasta, the Oedipal prize.*

When Orson Welles adapts an existing literary work, he endeavors to bring more nobility to the characters; he manifestly refuses to show shabby behavior on the screen, no doubt because he detests shabbiness more than anyone; this trait may likewise be one of the numerous aspects of the enormous Shakespearean influence on his manner of seeing and making one see.

Over the past few years, Orson Welles has been less reticent about personal confidences. When he told Jeanne Moreau, in the

---

*In his *Orson Welles,* Maurice Bessy informs us that Dr. Bernstein, who took over Orson's education after his mother's death, had been "passionately in love with her."

course of an interview on French television, that Booth Tarkington was a friend of his parents and that the portrait of the automobile pioneer Eugene Morgan was modeled after his own father, who had devoted his life to inventing harmless practical gadgets, a good many of our intuitions were confirmed: no one could dispute that the vain and possessive Amberson boy is a twin brother of the young Charles Foster Kane. One might even claim that as *Citizen Kane* shows us Charlie at eight, then at twenty-five, this large ellipsis in the first film is filled in the second by the evolution of the Amberson youth. "This kid needs a lesson and he's gonna get more than one" is a retort common to the dialogue of both films.*

With forty-three minutes amputated by RKO after one or more disappointing previews, *The Magnificent Ambersons* is a mutilated masterpiece. It hasn't had the repercussions of *Citizen Kane;* and in any theatre today, moreover, there will be half as many spectators for *Ambersons.* Yet each time I see this film it has a greater emotional effect on me. I believe that in shooting *Citizen Kane* Orson Welles was more anxious about the medium, while in *Ambersons* he seems to have been excited primarily by the characters. If someone should ever draw up a catalog of the cinema of sensibility, *The Magnificent Ambersons* should figure prominently next to Jean Vigo.

In 1942 we come to *Journey into Fear,* whose credits show us for the third and last time the beautiful graphics of Mercury Productions: large sunken letters in a classical design. For film-lovers today, the principal pleasure offered by this movie lies in the renewed acquaintance with Joseph Cotten, Ruth Warrick, Agnes Moorehead and Everett Sloane, not to mention the resurrection of Richard Bennett, the Major whom one had left for dead by his fireside, after the most beautiful scene in *Ambersons.*

As with Carol Reed's *The Third Man,* some perfectly executed

---

*Joseph McBride's excellent book *Orson Welles* reveals an astonishing and exciting fact. In the course of numerous preliminary rehearsals with his actors, Orson had recorded all the film's dialogue with the intention of shooting the entire film to synchronize with the playback. After shooting started he had to give up this idea, which presented too many technical difficulties for the actors.

scenes can be attributed without hesitation to Welles; the rest, unhappily, reverts to Norman Foster, the credited director.

Journey into Fear isn't entirely satisfying but it does contain certain beauties, and more humor than any other Orson Welles film, probably because the Eric Ambler subject doesn't lend itself to a lyrical treatment.

Of all Welles' films, *The Stranger* (1946), based on a script by Victor Trivas and Anthony Veiller (John Huston?), is the easiest to summarize afterward. I suspect that this should be attributed to the producer, Sam Spiegel, known during that period as Sam P. Eagle, doubtless to indicate that he envisaged himself flying high; the future producer of *The Bridge on the River Kwai* was probably already taking a hand in the preparation of scripts, with simplification in mind. This film—about the last days of a Nazi war criminal hiding in Connecticut, from his marriage under his new identity until his death, after he has been unmasked—is very clearly influenced by Hitchcock's *Shadow of a Doubt*. The same realistic and everyday portrait of a small town in America; the same succession of peaceful, familiar and familial scenes presented in contrast to the central character's terrible secret; the same construction on the principle of the vise closing in. One even finds the ladder rungs sawed through with the intention of making the heroine fall! Despite its considerable qualities, *The Stranger* is less distinguished, less dazzling than the other films of Orson Welles. Linearity probably doesn't suit him, and in his next film this would incite him to shuffle his deck of cards.

At the time of its release, *The Lady from Shanghai* was glowingly received by the film-lovers of my generation, and some of us even ranked it as high as *Citizen Kane*, probably because pure movie fans like to oppose the hierarchy of genres and prove that a "B" thriller can surpass a "big theme." Adapting a novel—a really feeble one—by Sherwood King, Orson Welles contrived to save the film scene by scene, transforming each episode into a showpiece. The only *raison d'être* of *The Lady from Shanghai* is . . . the cinema itself; and since Orson Welles is behind the camera that's already saying a lot, even if the spectator doesn't experience the emotion that he felt while watching *Kane* and *Ambersons.*

What remain most remarkable in the film over the years are the performances of the two actors playing the "villains": Everett Sloane as Rita Hayworth's husband, the great lawyer Arthur Bannister, who moves about supported by two canes, and Glenn Anders in the part of George Grisby, who sets a terrible trap for the innocent, ingenuous and amorous lead, Orson Welles himself.

Seeing the film again, one realizes that the screenplay is much simpler than it seems: the whole story is circumscribed by a journey from New York to San Francisco (by boat) by way of the Caribbean with a stopover in Acapulco! The script is very professional; each scene ends with a visual or sound gag and the action never stands still.

Visually the film is superb, and I agree with Bazin when he says: "Had he made only *Citizen Kane, The Magnificent Ambersons* and *The Lady from Shanghai,* Orson Welles would still deserve a prominent place among the citations carved on any Arch of Triumph celebrating the history of cinema."

Welles had made *The Lady from Shanghai* to show Hollywood that he was capable of making an ordinary film, but he demonstrated the reverse, not least to himself! It seems probable that in propos-/ ing a *Macbeth* to be shot in twenty-six days, he decided in effect to assume his position as an avant-garde director.

Thus *Macbeth*—with which Welles rediscovered freedom, poverty and his own genius, all intact—inaugurated the Shakespearean trilogy. No one has described this film better than Jean Cocteau: "Orson Welles' *Macbeth* has a kind of crude, irreverent power. Clad in animal skins like motorists at the turn of the century, horns and cardboard crowns on their heads, his actors haunt the corridors of some dreamlike subway. . . ."

The element of fairy tale or fable is particularly suited to the notion of a closed universe. Preserving the character and charm of the closed universe meant avoiding locations as documentary and antifictional intrusions—the real sky, the sun, all the natural and eternal elements which would register like sour notes in an orchestra. On the other hand, all the elements of décor which make our everyday life theatrical—doors, windows, ceilings and particularly door and window frames—are welcome because they visually reinforce the sense of "Once upon a time . . ."

In *Macbeth*, this closed-universe principle functions perfectly: artificial dampness seeps out of the coarse canvas material imitating high rocks; helmets and weapons are fashioned out of a primitive and barbarous scrap iron; the smoke machine emits a fog which diffuses and dramatizes the light—everything is savage in this film whose strength is that it doesn't contain a single shot filmed in natural locations.

It is also in *Macbeth* that Welles pushes to its most extreme a style of acting doubtless derived from his staging of Shakespeare in the theatre and which he gradually introduced into his films, chiefly *The Stranger* and *The Lady from Shanghai.* This involves the character that he plays walking toward the camera but not in its axis, proceeding like a crab while looking the other way; the eyes are almost never focused directly on the eyes of the other actor but somewhere above his head, as if the Wellesian hero could only converse with the clouds. The expression in the eyes is also quite special, seeming at once distracted and melancholy, sorrowfully preoccupied, suggesting that secret thoughts lie behind the words spoken. This style of acting, slightly hallucinated and quite unique, carries an unmatched poetic force. One is so accustomed to thinking of Orson Welles as a strong personality that one all too often forgets that he is also a remarkable actor.

Later, after having given up playing youthful leads, Orson Welles would inflate—I can't think of another word—this style of acting in others: Charlton Heston in *Touch of Evil,* Anthony Perkins in *The Trial.*

Welles has described in interviews how he shot *Othello,* in places many hundred of miles apart, improvising décors and costumes, using five or six different kinds of film stock, filming the backs of hooded figures doubling for actors called away to work on other films. Only the very great technician that he was from the beginning could have brought it off, and there is no doubt that in editing this film which comprises nearly two thousand shots (*Citizen Kane* had only 562, *Ambersons* probably only half that many), Welles became passionately involved with this stage of film-making. Welles has always been a musical director, but before *Othello* he created music *within* the shots. Starting with *Othello,* he would make music at the editing table, that is to say, *between* the shots. If *Othello* is so fragmented, this is because the transition from one shot to the next is accomplished sometimes by matching movements, sometimes by textual bridges, and sometimes by the inflections of voice or eye.

The first extended take in the film occurs when Iago, walking beside Othello, begins to sow doubts in his mind; the camera precedes both of them in a very long dolly across the ramparts. Michael MacLiammoir is remarkable in the role of Iago, and from the manner in which Welles highlights him in relation to both the camera and himself, one feels all the admiration, gratitude and respect he must have felt for the great Irish actor who gave him his start in 1931 at the Gate Theatre in Dublin, and who had pretended to believe that this young American tyro, sixteen years old and claiming to be twenty-five, was a great New York actor!

If *Othello* wasn't sufficiently admired at the time of its release, this is because, turning his back on Eisensteinian solemnity and the academic, stilted approach of Laurence Olivier, refusing to succumb to the "grand manner," Orson Welles sought to make not so much a masterpiece as a *living* film. In shooting *Othello* like a thriller—fastening it, in other words, to a popular genre—it seems to me that Orson Welles got closer to Shakespeare. I'm not unaware that this latter statement could get me turned back at the London airport. At the time, however, Welles himself declared: "The famous Shakespearean tradition that is so often invoked is more legend than dogma. In fact, it isn't a tradition at all; it's much too frequently a simple accumulation of bad habits."

The importance of editing! It is under this banner that we again find Orson Welles in *Mr. Arkadin (Confidential Report),* one of my favorite films, probably because here Welles uses the whole range of his keyboard. When he shot this film with an impoverished budget, Orson Welles had been making movies for fifteen years, and he devoted himself to a sort of recapitulation of his work. As Jean-Luc Godard would have said when he was a film critic: *Citizen Kane* + Shakespeare + Santa Claus = *Mr. Arkadin!*

In *Citizen Kane* Welles discovered the meaning of old age; in *Arkadin* he experiences it, and this is what creates the emotional impact, not only when we watch Arkadin himself, but also when we see Jacob Zouk, magnificently played by Akim Tamiroff. Equally magnificent are Michael Redgrave, the child-woman Paola Mori, [Frédéric] O'Brady, Mischa Auer, Patricia Medina and Katina Paxinou, who, in the role of Baroness Sophia Nagel, becomes the spitting image of another baroness whom Welles admired, Baroness Karen Blixen [Isak Dinesen], the brilliant Danish writer whose *Immortal Story* he would later adapt. Since Welles' entire life unfolds under the signs of coincidences and chance encounters, it will come as a surprise to no one that the same Karen Blixen, at the beginning of her novel *The Angelic Avengers,* written in Denmark in 1943, quotes the first lines of the poem by Coleridge which were paraphrased at the beginning of *Citizen Kane,* filmed by Welles four years earlier:

> In Xanadu did Kubla Khan
> A stately pleasure dome decree . . .
> So twice five miles of fertile ground
> With walls and towers were girdled round . . .

Gregory Arkadin has no fabulous palace, but the character is truly magical: he seems capable of being at one and the same time in Munich, Mexico, Istanbul. The witnesses to his past die one after the other thousands of miles apart just as the young Van Stratten, hired by Arkadin himself to find them, has discovered their whereabouts! The striking contrasts between décors, places, behaviors, personalities and ways of dying correspond to the principle of *enumeration,* which governs the composition of most fairy tales. One knew Welles as a film-maker of ambiguity; here in this film where he hunts, like Charles Perrault's ogre, for seven-league boots, he has become the film-maker of ubiquity. (Many supposedly "international" films are made, but only those of Orson Welles are truly international in spirit.)

The name Arkadin is so lovely that for a long time I wondered where it came from, until one day I attended a performance of Chekhov's *The Seagull,* in which the character of the actress is called Irina Arkadina.

When the use of video cassettes becomes widespread and people watch the films they love at home, anyone who owns a copy of *Mr. Arkadin* will be lucky indeed.

Next we come to *Touch of Evil,* in which Orson Welles makes himself look old and ugly as though to demonstrate, through exaggeration, that he has once and for all given up playing youthful leads—even though at this point, in 1957, he was only forty-two.

André Bazin, who loved Orson Welles so much and understood him so well, died a few months after having seen *Touch of Evil.* Note, however, how much his description of Captain Quinlan could be applied to Falstaff as imagined by Welles: "An ex-alcoholic, ugly and obese, who resists the temptations of whiskey by sucking on candy bars, the archangel is now only a poor devil, his grotesque genius bent to the least noble of tasks." Conversely, while describing *Macbeth* and *Othello,* Bazin seems to be describing *Touch of Evil:* "We should not be surprised that Welles' two Shakespearean films are in fact two of the tragedies most consistent with this duality theme [of *The Beauty and the Beast*], nor in particular that his adaptations plead innocence for Macbeth, pity for Othello. It is not so much the grandeur of evil—although the grandeur is there—as the innocence in the sin, fault or crime."

Although Welles deliberately makes himself old in *Touch of Evil,* his camera takes on the ardor of a young man. Each shot reveals a love of cinema and a pleasure in making it.

In a great many Hollywood films, we listen to a grandiose score by Tiompkin or Max Steiner which becomes agitated and takes flight, laid over images which are hopelessly congealed and static. In *Touch of Evil,* we witness an inverse phenomenon: it is Welles' images which sing and take flight while Henry Mancini's score remains earthbound.

In the years following the release of *Touch of Evil,* the influence exercised by this film would frequently be confirmed; for instance, in Stanley Kubrick's notorious *A Clockwork Orange. Touch of Evil* confirms an idea which can be verified by *The Big Sleep, Kiss Me Deadly* and *Psycho:* filmed by an inspired director, the most ordinary thriller can become the most moving fairy tale. "All great art is abstract," says Jean Renoir.

I must confess I am not an admirer of *The Trial,* which, like a good many of Welles' films, was a commissioned work, but which he perhaps shot with a paralyzing respect, for it is no longer a question of a thriller to magnify but of a masterpiece of world literature, Franz Kafka's *The Trial.* Frequently, and despite the collapse of the Mercury Theatre after *Ambersons,* Welles has tackled his film work in the same spirit as the director of a theatre company: "This year we'll do a Shakespeare." That year, 1962, he did a Kafka. It was the most elaborate film that Welles had made in some time, at least in terms of the gigantic settings and the abundance of extras. The two reasons that I'd give for my disappointment—after noting, however, that the French critical response was generally excellent—are that Welles, who is so much at ease filming power, pride and dominion, maybe isn't equipped to show their opposites: weakness, humility, submission. Since his adolescence, his corpulence and size have naturally led him to play kings. One almost never sees Orson Welles eat or drive a car (except in *The Lady from Shanghai).* One often sees him stand up but never sees him sit down. The prestigious character calls for a prestigious *mise en scène:* in classical angle/reverse-angle editing, Greta Garbo filmed over her shoulder from behind is unthinkable.

Orson Welles is bigger than life, Kafka is smaller than life. This is why, filmed from the same angle as Gregory Arkadin or Charles Foster Kane, with the camera at floor level, Kafka's hero, played by Anthony Perkins, remains distant and scarcely touches us. As Jean Cocteau put it: "The poet is a bird who must sing in his genealogical tree." I have seen *The Trial* several times, and after impatiently awaiting each of Akim Tamiroff's scenes, I have come to the conclusion that the film would have been Kafkaesque and moving if the cast had all been made up of Central European Jewish actors.

The strong point of *The Trial* is, once again, the editing. It was during this period that Welles flatly declared: "For me, editing isn't an aspect of cinema, it is *the* aspect." Hitchcock or Bresson would say—or do say—the same thing, even if their ideas differ strongly in execution. In order to play around with the editing at his leisure, Welles delivered *The Trial* five months late, for he is a more self-critical film-maker than is believed. When he films, he works by instinct, full of élan and impetuosity; afterward, as though taking severe stock of his flights, he criticizes himself pitilessly on the editing table. If I may be permitted to quote myself, I will cite a sentence from an old piece of mine, in which I said: "The films of Orson Welles are shot by an exhibitionist and cut by a censor."

Having played censor myself and being inclined to suggest that *The Trial* was possibly directed by Elmyr de Hory, I won't dwell any further on this film, which Bazin perhaps might have loved and in which he certainly would have discovered beauties that have escaped me.

Falstaff (Chimes at Midnight; 1966) isn't a play by Shakespeare but a script by Welles, put together from four plays by his favorite author. Previously, in 1939, Welles had done an adaptation of four plays for the stage (including, as here, *Henry IV* and *Richard III)* which he had called *Five Kings.* The show was apparently a flop, while here in *Falstaff* everything works wonderfully, thanks to the idea of centering everything around the character of Falstaff, whom Orson Welles plays superbly. When he saw Marcel Pagnol's film *The Baker's Wife* during the war, Welles had declared, "Raimu is the greatest actor in the world," and this remark comes back to me when I see this Falstaff, to whom Welles has given a Pag-

21

nolesque humanity. Supporting Welles-Falstaff, a number of excellent actors give the best of themselves: Jeanne Moreau, Keith Baxter, Margaret Rutherford, Fernando Rey, John Gielgud, Walter Chiari; the casting here is as harmonious as that of *Arkadin*. Edmond Richard's black-and-white photography is extraordinary, and the handling of camera and sound is little short of sublime.

About the next film I have only one complaint: its brevity. *Immortal Story* lasts only fifty minutes and consequently has received only limited distribution, although it tells a tale which might well have appealed to a wider audience. In the puritanical—or at any rate very chaste—work of Orson Welles, it offers us the first female nude, Jeanne Moreau, in the service of a sort of Arabian Nights tale written by a Dane and set in China!

What has always interested Orson Welles isn't psychology or thrillers or the romances and adventure stories that have been made since the cinema began; no, what interests him are stories in the form of tales, fables, allegories. Orson Welles, all of whose films implicitly begin with "Once upon a time . . . ," would be the best director to film *The Arabian Nights*.

It isn't surprising that he has a taste for Karen Blixen, the admirable Danish storyteller whom I had never even heard of until learning of her existence from Orson Welles himself during our only encounter, on an airplane.

Immortal Story is at once a story and the *mise en scène* of a story, since it is about the wealthy Macao merchant Mr. Clay (Orson Welles) planning to finance the realization in life of a very brief but powerful love story told by sailors as though it had actually happened to one of them. This story concerns a rich old man who, in order to have a child, pays a sailor five guineas to spend one night of love with his wife. When he hears it told by his secretary, Elishama, Mr. Clay wants this story to become true and so he recruits a prostitute, Virginia (Jeanne Moreau), and a sailor, in order to couple them within the space of a few hours. The day after the night of love, which has been splendid and intense "like an earthquake," Mr. Clay dies in his armchair.

Here we have "Once upon a time . . ." raised to the second power, and this film, made on a tiny budget, is one of Welles' most deeply felt. All the characters are sympathetic and touching. The story, depending upon Mr. Clay's fortune and the strength it gives him, pivots on conventional relations of power, but because each protagonist is willing and fulfilled, the tale elicits a sensation of melancholy sweetness. Welles and Jeanne Moreau are marvelous and the image of the sailor recruited by Mr. Clay, running in the streets behind the carriage, is unforgettable.

Taking over from François Reichenbach, who had made a documentary about the famous forger Elmyr de Hory, living in Ibiza, to whom Clifford Irving had devoted a book before becoming famous in turn for his fake Howard Hughes autobiography, Orson Welles has composed, in *F for Fake,* one of his films in which editing is paramount and the pseudo-documentary form serves as a vehicle for the poetry. Welles surely must have spent over a thousand hours making a thousand shots—certainly filmed in less time than that—sing together with one voice.

One of the final sequences shows us Picasso watching the beautiful Oja Palinkas as she strolls along the street. All the shots of the young woman are real and show her in movement; sometimes she is seen through the horizontal slats in gray window shutters. Is it Picasso who is watching the beautiful Yugoslav? Yes and no, for Orson Welles has cunningly filmed photographs of Picasso, portraits in which the eyes of the great painter are alert and looking to the left, to the right or directly into the lens. Sometimes sections of the shutters are found in front of Picasso's face and thus he seems to be spying on beautiful Oja, like a voyeur. This scene constitutes a superb demonstration of the possibilities of editing considered as a form of mystification—which is in fact the entire subject of this film, whose tall-tale mood and cynical liveliness lead us away from Shakespeare into something closer to Sacha Guitry. *F for Fake*—whose real subterranean purpose is probably a riposte to the controversy created by Pauline Kael—could have been called *La Romance des Tricheurs.* *

As I write [in July 1975], Orson Welles has made fifteen films, twelve of which have been shown to the public. What is happening with the other three?

Don Quixote, which was started nearly twenty years ago, has been voluntarily left incomplete by Welles, who shot and photographed it himself in various parts of the world, perhaps in 16mm, perhaps in 35mm (or perhaps alternating between the two). The cast includes Welles playing himself, the young Patty McCormick (by now probably old enough to be the mother of a family), and above all Akim Tamiroff, who died several years ago, conceivably without having completed his part. The reason given by Welles to explain the incompletion of the movie is the need to film, for the last scene, the explosion of the H-bomb which will destroy everything and everyone except for Don Quixote and Sancho Panza. Over the years, such a powerful legend has grown up around this film that it wouldn't be surprising if Welles preferred to remain its only spectator. Weary, besides, of being questioned so often about this film, Welles has decided to call it *When Are You Going to Finish Don Quixote?*

Deep Waters, based on a *série noire* thriller: Welles shot this film in 1967 in Yugoslavia and financed it himself, thanks to the enormous fee he was paid for playing in a patriotic Yugoslav blockbuster. The cast includes Jeanne Moreau, Laurence Harvey (who died shortly after having completed the dubbing of his part), Orson Welles himself and Oja Palinkas, a beautiful young Yugoslav actress who was to reappear in Welles' subsequent films. It derives from a good novel by Charles Williams, † an adventure-mystery involving the passengers on two separate boats. The film was shot with a very minimal crew, Welles handling the camera himself (except when he was acting), and Jeanne Moreau having assumed, in addition to her part, the job of script girl. Welles'

---

*A pun on the title of Guitry's film *Le Roman d'un Tricheur* (The Novel of a Trickster). (*Trans.*)

†*Dead Calm.* (*Trans.*)

reason for not showing the film is the absence of the final shot: the explosion at sea of one of the boats. Personally, I hope Welles will succeed in filming an explosion so grandiose that he'll consider it worthy to serve as the finale of *Don Quixote* as well!

As can be seen, the recent work of Orson Welles can be taken as a reflection on the cinema. Mr. Clay in *Immortal Story* indulges himself with the *mise en scène* of a story that pleases him, and dies as a result. The inquiry of *Fake* shows that a master film-planner in the editing room must be a master flim-flammer, and it was logical that Welles would wind up speaking directly about cinema in a movie.

Indeed, it turns out that the new film, *The Other Side of the Wind* —which Welles is completing at the moment I write—tells the story of an old Hollywood director who is shooting, or has just shot, his last movie. Filming began in summer 1970, then Welles stopped and started again several times in the manner inaugurated with *Othello*. Not wishing to be identified with the central character, Orson Welles hesitated a long time before choosing an actor for the part of the director, Hannaford; thus he filmed scenes while "fragmenting" them copiously, postponing the shots of Hannaford until later. In the spring of 1974, he decided to entrust his confrere John Huston with the Hannaford part.

This film should therefore not be taken as a farewell to the cinema—the equivalent of *The Testament of Orpheus* for Jean Cocteau—except insofar as in Welles' *oeuvre* one film in four has testamentary elements, starting with *Citizen Kane* and continuing in *Mr. Arkadin* and *Don Quixote;* one notes Welles' taste for biographies, existential balance sheets, dives into the past. It is easy to predict that he will have a lot to say to us about Hollywood, movie fans, biographers, reporters. . . . I believe that in the course of the film, Hannaford even speaks ironically about the number of books which have been devoted to him! And elsewhere, a nice line of dialogue is given to one character: "Did you know they had dissolves in Shakespeare?"

In my opinion, all the difficulties that Orson Welles has encountered with the box office, which have certainly put the brakes on his creative élan, stem from the fact that he is a film poet. The Hollywood financiers (and, to be fair, the public throughout the world) accept beautiful prose—John Ford, Howard Hawks—or even poetic prose—Hitchcock, Roman Polanski—but have much more difficulty accepting pure poetry, fables, allegories, fairy tales. There is no point in congratulating Welles for remaining faithful to himself and not making concessions, since he couldn't have done otherwise, even if he wanted to! Each time he says "Action!" he transforms vile reality into poetry.

However, Orson Welles has made films with his right hand (*Kane, Ambersons,* the three Shakespeare adaptations, *Immortal Story, The Other Side of the Wind*) and films with his left hand (the thrillers). In the right-handed films there is always snow, and in the left-handed ones there are always gunshots; but all constitute what Cocteau called the "poetry of cinematography."

For me, the real tragedy of Welles is that for thirty years he spent so much time with all-powerful producers who offered him cigars, but wouldn't have given him a hundred feet of celluloid to expose. They are the people who have hired him thirty times, possibly more, for parts lasting a few days in which he was "directed" (!) by film-makers one tenth as gifted. Furthermore, it is a matter of record that David Lean had ten months in which to shoot *Dr. Zhivago,* while Welles shot *Touch of Evil* in five weeks!

If one thinks of this aspect of his career, it is obvious that he must have forged a strong personal philosophy, never to have let fall in public one complaint, one harsh word, one sour thought or bitter remark.

In the idea that the film world has of Orson Welles, there is an "out of competition" and outsider aspect which must sometimes prove useful and help him in his creation and at other times obstruct and wound him. This may explain his celebrated "reluctant releases," whose proportions grow from year to year.

Orson Welles' career is therefore problematic, but no more so than that of Carl Dreyer or Jean Cocteau, and his activity as a successful actor, his star personality, certainly remove some urgency from the search for financial backing which is the lot of all film-makers. If he wasn't a great actor, if he wasn't constantly asked to play in the films of others, would Welles have shot more films as a director? I am inclined to think so, but his *oeuvre* is considerable in any case, and we must not forget that where the silent cinema gave us great visual talents—Murnau, Eisenstein, Dreyer, Hitchcock—the sound cinema has given us only one, one single film-maker whose style is immediately recognizable after three minutes of film, and his name is Orson Welles.

This is certainly what André Bazin has demonstrated in writing that: "With Orson Welles, [technique] . . . isn't merely a way of placing the camera, sets and actors [*mettre en scène*]; it places the very nature of the story in question. With this technique, the cinema strays a little further from the theatre, becomes less a spectacle than a narrative. Indeed, as in the novel, it isn't only the dialogue, the descriptive clarity . . . but the style imparted to the language which creates meaning."

François Truffaut
On the plane between Paris and Los Angeles

Profile of Orson Welles

by Jean Cocteau

I met Orson Welles in 1936 at the end of my world tour. It was in Harlem, at his *Black Macbeth,* a strange and wonderful spectacle to which Glenway Westcott and Monroe Wheeler had taken me. Orson Welles was still a very young man. *Macbeth* was again to reunite us at the Venice Festival in 1948. Oddly enough, I did not connect the young man of the Negro *Macbeth* with the famous director who was going to show me another *Macbeth* (his film) in a little cinema on the Lido. It was he who reminded me, in a Venice bar, of the remark I had once made to him that while in the theatre the sleepwalking scene was generally made little of, it was, to my mind, the essential scene.

Orson Welles' *Macbeth* is a *film maudit,* in the noble sense of the word, such as we used it to light the beacon of the Festival at Biarritz.*

Orson Welles' *Macbeth* leaves the spectator deaf and blind and I can well believe that the people who like it (and I am proud to be one) are few and far between. Welles shot the film very quickly

*Cf. Bazin's Preface. (*Trans.*)

after numerous rehearsals. In other words, he wanted it to retain a certain theatrical style, as proof that cinematography can put any work of art under its magnifying glass and dispense with the rhythm commonly supposed to be that of *cinéma*. I disapprove of the abbreviation *cinéma* because of what it represents. In Venice, again and again, we heard the absurd leitmotif: "It's cinematic" or "It isn't cinematic." And even: "This film is a good film, but it isn't cinematic" or "This isn't a good film, but it is cinematic." You can imagine how amusing we found this, and when interviewed together on the radio, Welles and I replied that we should love to know what a *cinematic film* was and that we asked only to be taught the recipe in order to put it into practice.

Orson Welles' *Macbeth* has a kind of crude, irreverent power. Clad in animal skins like motorists at the turn of the century, horns and cardboard crowns on their heads, his actors haunt the corridors of some dreamlike subway, an abandoned coal mine, and ruined cellars oozing with water. Not a single shot is left to chance. The camera is always placed just where destiny itself would observe its victims. Sometimes we wonder in what period this nightmare is unfolding, and when, for the first time, we see Lady Macbeth, before the camera moves back to situate her, it is almost a woman in modern dress that we are seeing, reclining on a fur-covered divan beside the telephone.

In the role of Macbeth, Orson Welles proves himself to be a remarkable tragedian, and if the Scottish accent imitated by Americans may be unbearable to English ears, I confess that it did not disturb me and that it would not have disturbed me even if I had a perfect command of English, since we have no reason not to expect that strange monsters express themselves in a monstrous language in which the words of Shakespeare nevertheless remain his words.

In short, I am a poor judge and a better judge than others in that, without any difficulty, I could concentrate on the plot alone and my discomfort arose from it instead of from a faulty accent.

The film, withdrawn by Welles from the competition in Venice and screened by *Objectif 49*, in 1949, at the Salle de la Chimie, has everywhere met with the same kind of opposition. It epitomizes the character of Orson Welles, who disregards convention and whose weaknesses, to which the public clings as to a life preserver, have alone afforded him any success. Sometimes his boldness is blessed with such good fortune that the public is willing to be seduced, as, for example, in the scene from *Citizen Kane* when Kane wrecks the bedroom, or in that of the maze of mirrors from *The Lady from Shanghai.*

And yet, after the syncopated rhythm of *Citizen Kane,* the public expected a succession of syncopes and was disappointed by the calm beauty of *The Magnificent Ambersons.* It was easier for the soul to go astray in the labyrinthine penumbra taking us from the strange image of the little millionaire, not unlike Louis XIV, to the hysterics of his aunt.

Welles the student of Balzac, Welles the psychologist, Welles reconstructing old American mansions: this is what the fanatics of jazz and jitterbug found so shocking. They rediscovered Welles with the rather confused *Lady from Shanghai,* lost him again with *The Stranger,* and this roller coaster brings us to the moment when Orson Welles came from Rome to live in Paris.

Orson Welles is a kind of giant with the look of a child, a tree filled with birds and shadow, a dog that has broken its chain and lies down in the flower beds, an active idler, a wise madman, an island surrounded by people, a pupil asleep in class, a strategist who pretends to be drunk when he wants to be left in peace.

He knows better than anyone how to use the apparent nonchalance of true strength to give an impression of drifting, and advances with a half-open eye. The derelict manner he sometimes affects, like some dozing bear, shields him from the cold, restless whirl of the film world. A method that made him pack his bags, leave Hollywood and allow himself to be drawn toward other company and other prospects.

When I left Paris for New York, the morning of my departure Orson Welles sent me an automaton, an admirable white rabbit that could move its ears and play the drum. It brought to my mind the drum-playing rabbit of which Apollinaire speaks in the preface to the Picasso-Matisse exhibition at the Paul Guillaume gallery and which symbolized for him the sort of surprise that awaits us at the bend of a road.

This magnificent toy was the real sign, the real signature of Welles, and whenever an Oscar, representing a lady poised on tiptoe, arrives from America, or in France I am awarded the little Victory of Samothrace, I think of Orson Welles' white rabbit as the Oscar of Oscars and as my true Prize.

The idiom of cinematography, I repeat, is not one of words. When I first screened *Les Parents Terribles* in the San Marco cinema at Venice, outside the festival proper—from which I should have withdrawn *L'Aigle à Deux Têtes*, as he had withdrawn *Macbeth*—we were seated side by side. He could not have understood all the text; but at the least nuance in *mise en scène*, he would squeeze my arm with all his strength. It was poorly projected and, because the lighting was too weak, one could not clearly distinguish faces, so important in a film like this. As I was making apologies for this, he told me that the beauty of a film escaped ears and eyes and did not depend on dialogue, or machines, that even with poor projection and poor sound it should not be possible to harm its rhythm.

I agree with him. Sometimes, in *The Magnificent Ambersons*, for example, he will develop this idea to the point of using unattractive photography as an antidote to charm. But after *Les Parents Terribles*, at the Café Florian on the Piazza San Marco, we agreed that one must not fall from one charm into another nor calculate in advance the aura of patina, which would amount to painting instantaneous old pictures.

In fact, neither Welles nor I enjoy speaking about our work. The spectacle of life itself prevents us. We might remain a long time without moving and watch the hotel stir around us. Our immobility would demoralize busy businessmen and frantic specialists of cinematography. It resembled the ordeal of a gondola when busy businessmen and frantic specialists have to climb in and submit to its rhythm. Very soon we were receiving menacing looks. Our stillness had us taken for spies. Our silence caused fright and was charged with explosives. If we happened to laugh, it was frightful.

31

I would see solemn gentlemen pass at top speed in front of us for fear of being tripped up. We were accused of *lèse-festival,* of keeping to ourselves.

It was all so unreal, so close to collective hypnosis, that Welles and I never manage to meet in Paris.

His movements are on one side, mine on the other. If he should enter a restaurant, the manager informs him that I have just left, and vice versa. We loathe the telephone. In short, our encounters have become what they should be: a miracle. And this miracle always happens when it should.

I leave to Bazin the task of speaking to you in detail of a multiple work which is not limited to cinematography, in which journalism, the Martian practical joke, the stage productions of *Julius Caesar* and *Around the World in 80 Days,* have an important place. I wanted to sketch the profile of a friend whom I like and whom I admire, which is to repeat myself as far as Orson Welles is concerned, since my liking and my admiration are one.

August 1949

Jean Cocteau
Translated by Gilbert Adair

Preface

======✐======

The Renaissance of the American Cinema

======✐======

For all film-lovers who had reached the age of cinematic reason by 1946, the name of Orson Welles is identified with the enthusiasm of rediscovering the American cinema; still more, he epitomizes the conviction, shared by every young critic at the time, of being present at a rebirth and a revolution in the art of Hollywood. *Citizen Kane* represented for that postwar period a little of what *The Cheat* represented for 1914–1918, except that Cecil B. De Mille's film illustrated the beginnings of an art which had long since ceased to stammer in 1941. But it was once again a profound innovation in style and language which seemed then to constitute the importance of Welles' first film, even more than the audacity of the subject. Writing in *La Revue du Cinéma* that "One may wonder whether Orson Welles doesn't deserve to be ranked after Griffith, Chaplin, Stroheim, Eisenstein in the history of the cin-

As André S. Labarthe explains in his preface to the French edition, Bazin's manuscript contained no chapter or section divisions or headings; all these have been supplied by the French publisher. (*Trans.*)

ema," Jacques Doniol-Valcroze was expressing the opinion of many critics—certainly of all those who shortly thereafter grouped themselves around Jean Cocteau, Robert Bresson and Roger Leenhardt to found *Objectif 49,* whose memorial manifesto was the Festival du Film Maudit at Biarritz. Orson Welles might well have served as the honorary president of this movement, which saw itself as being pointed resolutely toward the future.

Looking back after more than ten years on my enthusiasm at the time, I naturally ask myself how much of it remains and whether we deceived ourselves in making the author of *Citizen Kane* the symbol of our hopes for the revitalizing of the cinema. Frankly, I don't think so, even if in the following pages I should happen to modify some of my former judgments or rectify the relative importance that I now accord to this or that technical and stylistic audacity.

First of all, we didn't deceive ourselves in 1946 by showing our admiration for a film of 1940.* Hindsight only confirms it. The forties were clearly the critical years of development for Hollywood, a fact revealed to us only after the war. The previous decade is characterized by the maturity and apotheosis of the great genres that were the glory of American talkies: the psychological and choreographical comedy, the gangster film, slapstick and zany comedy (Laurel and Hardy, the Marx Brothers), and of course the Western. Around 1937, Hollywood production assuredly reached a high point of perfection and, above all, equilibrium—in short, classicism. All the historical conditions were present for a slide into decadence, if a few brilliant or at least deeply original works hadn't arrived to regenerate inspiration and technique, shaking up practices which were already becoming conventions, provoking one of those mutations of taste that lie behind all new artistic currents. France had *La Règle du Jeu;* Hollywood, *Citizen Kane.* It would of course be saying too much to credit the rebirth of the American cinema entirely to Welles' notorious film. It is simply a question

---

*The delay of *Citizen Kane* in reaching France is, of course, attributable to the ban placed on American films under the Vichy government and German occupation. *(Trans.)*

of seeing it as the most significant and certainly the most effective blow that shook the pillars of the temple. And not only from a negative point of view, but positively: a stylistic and intellectual contribution, vast and fruitful. Nicholas Ray, who is the American director most representative of the fifties resurgence—the wave that also includes Richard Brooks, Robert Aldrich, Anthony Mann and Elia Kazan—has declared: "[Welles] is one of the greatest directors in the history of the cinema, and all of us who try to direct movies owe him a debt for the many new paths he pioneered. . . . He is a great man of the Theatre—and don't let anybody tell you otherwise."*

Thus, ten years later, the opinion of an American film-maker of the new generation matches that of the young French critics of 1946–1950, confirming that they were right to single out Orson Welles' work as one of the most authentic expressions of the cinematic avant-garde just after the war. Had he made only *Citizen Kane*, *The Magnificent Ambersons* and *The Lady from Shanghai*, Orson Welles would still deserve a prominent place among the citations carved on any Arch of Triumph celebrating the history of cinema.

*Reported by Peter Noble in *The Fabulous Orson Welles.*

Initial Forays:
Theatre and Radio

The Child Prodigy

Orson Welles was born on May 6, 1915, in Kenosha, Wisconsin, not far from Chicago, to a prosperous and imaginative family combining a heredity of art and technology. His father, Richard Head Welles, was at one and the same time an inventor, an industrialist and a hotelier; his mother, Beatrice Ives Welles, a well-known pianist. From Orson's earliest infancy, the family milieu assured him the company of artists and intellectuals—actors, painters, writers, musicians—friends of his parents, who didn't believe in sending children off to bed or to eat with the servants when there were visitors. Mr. and Mrs. Welles were rather in the style of Montaigne's father. Their son accordingly retains a grateful and tender memory of their intelligent benevolence. "My father," he says, "was a gentle, sensitive soul whose kindness, generosity and tolerance made him much beloved by all his friends. To him I owe the advantage of not having a formal education until I was ten years old. From him I inherited the love of travel, which has become ingrained within me. From my mother I inherited a real and lasting love of music and the spoken word, without which no human being is really a complete and satisfactory person." However one interprets the work of Orson Welles, one would therefore be wrong to contrive to see any revolt against an unhappy or beleaguered childhood, unless it was some purely paradoxical revolt against this happiness. Perhaps the adult who hasn't suffered at the age when kids have nightmares is also incomplete.

Be that as it may, Orson Welles' parents placed no restriction on the precocious manifestations of his genius. Had they given birth to an ordinary child, they would in any case have provided him with that refined liberal education in which the precosity of the young prodigy was given the power to explode. His explosions carried as far as the local press, since one finds an article about Orson in a Madison, Wisconsin, newspaper, with the headline: "Cartoonist, Actor, Poet—and only Ten!" But for several years he had already been known as a child prodigy at the Washington School in Madison, run by a well-known psychologist and teacher named Mueller. The latter had discovered that his pupil was an ideal, quite exceptional subject for multiple tests, which confirmed a mental age that was monstrously advanced. Anecdotes exist about his stay at the Washington School that are worthy of the little genius at the progressive school depicted by Chaplin in *A King in New York*. Dr. Bernstein, who was a friend of the parents before becoming the orphan's guardian, has written to Peter Noble, the English biographer of Orson Welles (from whom this chapter borrows a great deal).

> I was astounded by the extraordinary mental maturity of the boy. He was talking remarkably sound sense at the age of two, and I felt sure, from his appearance, demeanour and receptivity to paintings and sculptures, that he was destined to be some kind of an artist. Since his mother was such a talented pianist, I guessed the child would be musical, so I gave Orson a violin on his third birthday. Unfortunately his arms were too short for him to attempt to play it. So I did the next best thing and bought him a conductor's baton.

It was the same Dr. Bernstein who had introduced his future ward to magic tricks. This instruction, as we know, wouldn't fall on deaf ears, and would lead him to saw Marlene Dietrich in half out of patriotism.* After the compleat illusionist's outfit, the good doctor gave Orson a puppet theatre, which was doubtless at the source of the boy's vocation for theatre, a vocation that would little by little, as we shall see, override his interest in music and drawing.

This scarcely conventional education didn't prevent Orson Welles from traveling with his parents. It was in the course of a trip to Europe that he lost his mother, when he was only eight. His widowed father retired from business and traveled even more, always taking along his son, who would visit almost all of Europe and a good part of Asia this way.

Later, when he wasn't in China or Jamaica, and after the death of his father, which unfortunately occurred a few years after that of his mother, Orson was taking courses at Todd, another school well known for its revolutionary methods. If he didn't really learn how to add or subtract, he did in fact complete his literary-theatrical education and began to exhibit, as an amateur, his qualities as a director and an actor. Roger Hill, director of Todd, allowed him to put on Elizabethan plays, and it was here that Orson first had the idea for that famous "digest" of several Shakespeare plays which he would later present with the Mercury Theatre under the title *Five Kings*. With a production of *Julius Caesar,* he eventually carried away a prize from the Chicago Drama League for the best high school production in the Chicago area, but not before the jury required formal proof that the actors weren't professionals.

When Orson Welles left the Todd School, he was sixteen and had five hundred dollars in his pocket. He still dreamed of perfecting his drawing and painting, but he especially wanted to travel and do theatre work. He set off for Europe and used as his jumping-off point the austere and picturesque isle of Aran, so dear to Flaherty. From Aran he proceeded naturally to Ireland. Dublin was a city with a rich theatrical tradition: it was here that the Wisconsin

*A reference to an act performed by Welles to entertain servicemen in *Follow the Boys* (Eddie Sutherland, 1944). *(Trans.)*

Wonder Boy, child prodigy and prodigal, would finally begin to astonish the world as a professional.

A Theatricality That Overflows the Stage

Before coming to Orson Welles' filmic activity, which is obviously our main interest here, let us linger a little further over his theatre work. If we don't feel that this subject should be treated too cursorily, this is because theatre not only precedes cinema for the director of *Citizen Kane* and *Othello,* but profoundly and essentially conditions all the manifestations of Welles' genius, the cinema first of all. We will see this, moreover, in greater detail when we analyze the *mise en scène* of the films he has directed. The immediate and obvious connections between Welles' theatre and his filmography suffice to justify this attention. Indeed, one cannot really understand *Macbeth* and *Othello* without reference to the stage experience of their director. But beyond the obvious relationships, and more essentially than through the choice of subjects, theatre informs many aspects of Welles' style internally. Even more, theatre is the determining factor, perhaps even in his life, but theatre understood in its broadest sense, as an impulse toward grand gestures, thus including even that taste for publicity and scandal which can irritate certain people. Theatre in the traditional sense of the word—more particularly, Elizabethan theatre—is unquestionably at the base of Orson Welles' culture and taste, but it is equally unquestionable that in his case *theatricality* overflows the stage and spills into life. When—as we shall shortly see—the government prevented the Federal Theatre from performing *The Cradle Will Rock* and the company found the doors of the theatre locked, Orson Welles improvised an entertainment in the street for the spectators, in formal evening attire, which afforded time to find a solution to the problem of an auditorium. When one was finally discovered, the sets were loaded onto trucks along with the actors. This amazing parade then set off, followed by the audience, until the entire procession arrived at the Old Venice Theatre, where the play's first night took place in spite of the Washington bureaucrats. I don't know what the critics praised most in the press the next day—the *mise en scène* of *The Cradle Will Rock* or that incredible improvisation on a city-wide scale which encompassed it: Orson Welles perched on a truck and mesmerizing the crowd like Mark Antony over the corpse of Caesar.

Dublin: First Roles

So in 1931, Orson at sixteen landed in Dublin (having first toured Ireland in a donkey cart), where he sat in amazement before a performance of a Synge play put on by the Gate Theatre. In its three years of existence, this excellent Irish company directed by Hilton Edwards and Michael MacLiammoir had acquired an international reputation. With splendid audacity, Orson introduced himself to the directors as a "star of the New York Theatre Guild." MacLiammoir relates:

> We found a very tall young man with a chubby face, full, powerful lips, and disconcerting Chinese eyes. . . . His voice, with its brazen Transatlantic sonority, was already that of a preacher, a leader, a man of power; it bloomed and boomed its way through the dusty air of the scene dock as though it would crush down the little Georgian walls and rip up the floor; he moved in a leisurely manner from foot to foot and surveyed us with magnificent patience as though here was our chance to do something beautiful at last—yes, sir—and were we going to take it?

He was indeed hired to play the part of Duke Alexander of Wurtemberg in *The Jew Süss*. Since this character is an old man of sixty, the teen-ager discovered here an opportunity to create one of those impersonations that he loved doing at the Todd School, and particularly to use makeup abundantly. Orson Welles' liking for false hair and makeup is well known and harks back to his early childhood. He was only ten or so when Dr. Bernstein discovered a disheveled Lilliputian old man with haggard eyes in his protégé's room: it was Orson rehearsing *King Lear*. There have been numerous performances since, in both plays and films, in which Orson

Welles has amused himself by remodeling his face and altering his age; but conversely, it is less often noted how rarely he has acted *without* false hair or makeup, particularly without remodeling his nose. He has explained this as follows:

> Both Laurence Olivier and I detest our own noses. They tend to give our faces a comic appearance, whereas we both have a strong desire to play mainly dramatic roles. At the drop of a hat Olivier clamps a false nose over his handsome proboscis, and I, too, strongly possess this tendency. For all normal uses, my own nose is quite pleasant and fairly decorative. It stopped growing, however, when I was about ten years old. Thus it is violently unsuitable for roles such as Lear, Macbeth and Othello.

One will note that this justification refers not only to his nose's shape but also to its childlike aspect. We will later be considering this obsession about childhood more seriously. But I also recall a conversation with Orson Welles in which he conjured up before me the pleasure of acting on the stage with a corrected nose. He didn't even invoke the exigencies of style, but rather the need of a mask, that little shield of cardboard or modeling paste which suffices to defend you from the public. Acting with an exposed nose is like approaching the footlights naked.

After *The Jew Süss*, Orson played the Ghost in *Hamlet* and the King of Persia in something called *Mogu of the Desert*.

Despite his relative inexperience and the extravagance of some of his performances, the young actor got sufficiently good notices for his reputation to reach London, where offers proliferated. Finally he left Dublin for England. Unfortunately, the Ministry of Labour refused to grant him a work permit and Welles had to return to America, though not without first paying a visit to Bernard Shaw.

Debut as a Director

But Broadway was a long way from Dublin, and there this "kid" wasn't taken seriously. Welles took advantage of his forced unem-

41

ployment to undertake—with advice from his friend Roger Hill of the Todd School—an annotated stage edition of Shakespeare's works, including numerous production notes and sketches by Welles himself. This work was assembled in a volume entitled *The Mercury Shakespeare*. Then he made his way to Morocco, where he devoted himself to painting, and to Spain, where he became enthusiastic about bullfighting and even ventured into the arena. After his return to Chicago, he languished for a few more months, only partially occupied by writing a biography of John Brown, until the day when a meeting with Thornton Wilder finally gained him a foothold in the American theatre by way of an introduction to the celebrated actress Katharine Cornell, who hired him to act in touring productions of *Romeo and Juliet, Candida* and *The Barretts of Wimpole Street,* and promised to give him a New York debut upon their return, in the role of Mercutio in *Romeo and Juliet.* In fact, he would only get the part of Tybalt. Between the end of this tour and the start of the new theatrical season, Welles amused himself in Woodstock by organizing and staging a sort of festival under the auspices of the Todd School, for which he brought his Gate Theatre friends Hilton Edwards and MacLiammoir over from Dublin. Excluding his amateur efforts, it was at the Todd School in 1934 that Welles made his real debut as a director.

The Woodstock Drama Festival has a further importance in Welles' biography: it was here that he made the acquaintance of a lovely eighteen-year-old actress, Virginia Nicholson, whom he married a few months later, at the age of nineteen. In 1939 the couple had a daughter, whom they named Christopher, having hoped for a son. In Katharine Cornell's company—where he didn't have the satisfaction of playing leading roles—Welles finally started to make himself known on Broadway. The producer of a young avant-garde theatre group, John Houseman, took notice of him and offered him work. The job in question was putting on a socially conscious and progressive verse play which dealt with the

Wall Street crash, Archibald MacLeish's *Panic.** The production had only three performances, but the Welles-Houseman association, which would last for several years, was born.† As a start, it would constitute the glory of the Federal Theatre.

The Federal Theatre was a very praise worthy initiative of Rooseveltian politics. To remedy the crisis in the theatre and particularly the unemployment which had been plaguing actors since 1933, Washington decided to subsidize theatrical companies in each state. In New York, there were no less than five companies, including the Negro Theatre, conducted by John Houseman. He naturally appealed to his friend Orson Welles, who in the meantime had been acquiring a name in radio, where his golden voice was performing miracles.

It was at this point that Welles had the idea of staging his famous black *Macbeth* by transposing the action from Scotland to Tahiti†† during the reign of the black emperor Jean Christophe, with the witches becoming voodoo sorcerers. "Our purpose," Orson Welles has written, "was not as capricious and foolish as it might sound. We wanted—indeed, we were anxious—to give to Negro artists, many of whom are very talented, an opportunity to play in the sort of thing that is usually denied them. The parts that fall to Negroes are too often old mammies with bandanas, water-melon-eating piccaninnies, Uncle Rastuses and so on." With Virgil Thomson's music and Nat Karson's costumes, this *Macbeth* was a memorable production, in which Orson Welles was able to display the extent of his inventiveness and establish his youthful authority.

After *Macbeth,* and again for the Federal Theatre, Welles staged *Horse Eats Hat,* a rather free version of *An Italian Straw Hat,* harking back to the René Clair film, which had deeply impressed him; then Marlowe's *Dr. Faustus.* During the same period he acted on another

---

*Bazin's implication that Welles directed *Panic* is erroneous; he played the role of McGafferty, but the direction was handled by Martha Graham and James Light. *(Trans.)*

†This association came to an end in December 1940 after the making of *Citizen Kane* and one more stage production directed by Welles, an adaptation of Richard Wright's *Native Son.*

††Another error: the action was transposed to Haiti. *(Trans.)*

43

Broadway stage in a play—as indigestible as it was idealistic—
attacking armament manufacturers, entitled *Ten Million Ghosts*.
This was a worthy flop, which didn't discourage Welles from putting on another social and progressive show for the Federal
Theatre: a sort of satire of American political life in the form of an
opera, entitled *The Cradle Will Rock*. This time the enemies of the
Federal Theatre and Rooseveltian politics achieved a more solid
position and Washington took notice. In the end, Welles and
Houseman received an order to abandon their opera. They
refused to obey, and the police closed the theatre on opening
night. Two thousand people remained in the street in front of the
locked doors, and it was for them that Orson Welles improvised
the marvelous demonstration we have already described. The Federal Theatre was dead, but the glory of Orson Welles had taken
another giant step forward.

The Mercury Theatre

In 1937 his reputation finally enabled Welles to create his own
company, again with Houseman. The two associates found a silent
partner without too much difficulty, and the Mercury Theatre was
born. Its originality lay in the ambition to present modern and
classical plays in repertory, which is done by several European
companies but was virtually unknown on Broadway, where the
general practice still is to keep plays running for several months.

The Mercury Theatre began by putting on *Julius Caesar*. Making
a virtue out of the low budget, Welles, who assumed the part of
Brutus, decided to play the Shakespeare tragedy in modern dress.
At the height of European fascism, this modernization had an
audacious impact. The play was performed, moreover, without
sets, using only a system of movable platforms set against the bare
bricks of the theatre's back wall. The opening of *Julius Caesar* on
November 11, 1937, caused a stir among the New York critics, who
were all the more unstinting in their enthusiasm since they could
use it the following day as a foil to the sumptuous and flashy
staging of *Antony and Cleopatra* with Tallulah Bankhead. The suc-

cess of *Julius Caesar* was such that the program had to be quickly revised. The production was moved to a larger and more central theatre, where it ran for several months before returning to the Mercury and was staged in repertory with a modern play by Thomas Dekker, *Shoemaker's Holiday.* * In the spring of 1938, the Mercury presented Bernard Shaw's *Heartbreak House,* in which Welles had fun portraying the octogenarian Captain Shotover. This difficult play was only moderately successful. Business wasn't too bad at this stage, but Welles didn't trouble himself about costs, and despite everything the company could be done in by one big commercial flop. This occurred with Büchner's *Danton's Death,* which Welles staged in a more extravagant manner than *Julius Caesar.* He had escalators of a certain sort built,† which made the actors lurch up onto the stage, and had seventeen hundred masks glued to the back wall to suggest the masses. The play was a worthy and distinguished flop despite Welles' performance as Saint-Just. Finally, the next project, in the spring of 1939, was a disaster: a synthesis of *Richard II, Henry IV, Henry V, Henry VI* and *Richard III* shamelessly titled *Five Kings.* Fifteen thousand dollars was still needed while rehearsals were going on, and *Five Kings* never opened.

The Mercury Theatre was dead! Long live the Mercury Theatre! Basically, this honorable demise after two years of glorious activity was something more than a failure. As brief as its life had been, the Mercury had played a major role in the prewar American theatre and its influence could be compared to that of the Cartel in France. But above all, from the point of view that concerns us here, it marked an essential plateau in Orson Welles' career. It was with the Mercury that, at the age of twenty-three, he was finally able to realize the full measure of his theatrical genius. It was also with the

---

*Scarcely modern; the play dates back to 1600. (*Trans.*)

†According to Peter Noble's *The Fabulous Orson Welles,* these were elevators. A more detailed and probably more accurate description of this construction—"a four-sided structure the centre of which was occupied by an elevator shaft through which a small platform travelled up and down, descending to the basement to unload and rising to a maximum height of twelve feet above the stage"—can be found in John Houseman's *Run-Through* (Simon and Schuster, 1972). (*Trans.*)

Mercury that Orson Welles continued to assemble that marvelous company of actors, nearly all of whom were to become famous and who would support him with such fine ensemble performances a little later in his work in Hollywood: Joseph Cotten, George Coulouris, Agnes Moorehead, Everett Sloane, Paul Stewart, Erskine Sanford, Ray Collins.

The end of the Mercury Theatre has brought us very close to the day when Hollywood sounded its trumpets for Orson Welles. If one wants to play at rewriting history, it isn't too difficult to imagine how the theatre would have led the brilliant Broadway director to the film capital in any event. It wouldn't have been the only such instance: particularly since the war, exchanges are frequent between Broadway and Hollywood, not only of scripts—which has always been the case in America—but also, and increasingly, of actors and directors. We know what the American cinema of the mid-fifties owes to Elia Kazan's famous Actors Studio,* from which emerged, notably, James Dean and Marlon Brando. Previously, playwrights like Clifford Odets and Thornton Wilder operated in Hollywood after having been the avant-garde of the New York theatre. Today, in addition to Elia Kazan, Hollywood owes some of the films that are the most interesting and the richest in promise for the health of the American cinema to Joshua Logan, one of the most famous Broadway directors. Welles would undoubtedly have landed in Hollywood someday, but it is highly probable that this would have been later and under very different conditions, which would not have left him the freedom occasioned by an extratheatrical fame acquired during three years on the radio and capped by the famous "Martian" broadcast.

Martians on the Airways

Orson Welles' radio experience has perhaps been no less decisive for his filmic work than his theatrical experience. To describe

*It was a common error in French criticism of this period to ascribe Lee Strasberg's Actors Studio to Elia Kazan. (*Trans.*)

it, therefore, is not merely to indulge in anecdotes. Since, however, it is even more famous and familiar than his dramatic successes, we can be relatively brief in our account of it. It is not generally known, though, to what extent the incredible adventure of the imaginary invasion of New Jersey by the Martians was unpremeditated.

Since his Federal Theatre days, Welles had been a star on the CBS network, where he had acquired more and more freedom. From 1938, he directed a weekly broadcast for CBS featuring his theatre group: *The Mercury Theatre on the Air.* This program offered each week an adaptation of a classic work, with Welles as the master of ceremonies. After *Treasure Island, Jane Eyre, The Man Who Was Thursday, Julius Caesar, Around the World in 80 Days* and some other broadcasts on subjects equally unscandalous, Welles had the idea of broadcasting a work of what we would today call science fiction. He first thought of books such as Shiel's *Purple Cloud* and Conan Doyle's *Lost World* before settling on *The War of the Worlds* by his near-namesake, H. G. Wells.

Initially, the book's material appeared so disappointing to the adapters that the broadcast almost failed to take place. They found these Martian adventures completely idiotic. But Orson, while conducting rehearsals of *Danton's Death,* had to face up to his radio contract and hardly had the leisure to change his program *in extremis.* On October 29, 1938, disheartened by the mediocrity of the recording of a trial run, Welles and his Mercury friends concluded that the only way to add a little flavor to the story was to emphasize the realism of the events in newscast style, and he spent the night revising the adaptation to give it more authenticity by situating the action in different parts of America. Nevertheless, the results didn't look like much, and this was also the opinion of all those who heard the final rehearsal, actors and technicians alike. But it was too late to make improvements.

The rest is history, and if the event hadn't left tangible traces and become the object of serious scientific studies, we would scarcely believe today that it happened, especially on such a scale. This extraordinary phenomenon of collective, nationwide schizophrenia would seem to be an inflated publicity gimmick or a figment of the Welles legend. But the facts are inescapable. An unidentified announcer broke in during the broadcast with prime news of the landing of Martians in New Jersey; then, from time to time, other communications of this sort, including a "dramatic" speech from the Secretary of the Interior; finally the President came on to confirm the gravity of the situation.* This was all it took for thousands, then hundreds of thousands and finally millions of listeners to believe that the end of the world had come. The consequences of this panic are celebrated: people fled in all directions, those from the city to the country and vice versa. In the dead of night, highways were streaked with innumerable cars. Priests were called to hear confessions. There were miscarriages, broken limbs in the scuffles, heart attacks; hospitals and psychiatric centers didn't know how to cope with the rush of patients. In Pittsburgh, a woman took her own life rather than let herself be violated by the Martians. In the South, people prayed together in public places. Looting began in half-abandoned cities. In New Jersey, the National Guard was called out. Several days—if not several weeks— later, Red Cross volunteers and Quakers were still going up into the Black Hills of Dakota, persuading the miserable, terrorized families that they could return to their homes. Along with Orson Welles, there was undoubtedly at least one beneficiary of this collective hysteria—the worthy Mr. Hadley Cantril, professor of psychosociology at Princeton University, who took delight in his subject and described it in a learned work as the "first modern panic that has been studied with the research tools now available to the social scientist."

While half of America was panic-stricken, while the police were surrounding the studio, whose telephone lines were jammed with incoming calls, Orson Welles was imperturbably continuing with this "mediocre" broadcast before dashing off with his actors to the theatre for the evening rehearsals for *Danton*. He was not really to

---

*This detail is erroneous. The President didn't figure in the broadcast. Cf. *The War of the Worlds* recording (Charisma Perspective) or the text of Howard Koch's radio play in *The Panic Broadcast* (Avon, 1970). *(Trans.)*

discover until the following morning, and to his great astonishment, the extent of the disaster—or of his triumph.

The consequences of this incredible panic were multiple and varied, and it is even probable that Orson Welles would have long repented of it if he hadn't had an excellent lawyer who was quite attentive to the wording of his contracts. The one that tied him to CBS happily left Welles free from responsibilities connected with the consequences of broadcasts, except in matters concerned with attempts at plagiarism or libel suits. So it was CBS that had to deal with over a good hundred lawsuits instituted by the victims of the mystification of October 30, 1938.

One final word, without prejudice to the explanations of the worthy Mr. Cantril of Princeton. It is worth remembering—if not to explain it, at least to situate it in its historical context—that this doubly Wellesian "end of the world" exploded in an America made sensitive by anxiety about the coming war. It was the period of Munich, and the day wasn't far away when an unidentified announcer would interrupt an entertainment broadcast to declare in a trembling voice that Pearl Harbor had just been destroyed by the Japanese. But this time, many Americans who had gone along with Welles would believe it to be a joke in bad taste.

October 30,1938. *The War of the Worlds*

Hollywood 1939–1941:
The Great Diptych

An Unprecedented Contract

This spectacular hullabaloo having finally raised Welles to the status of a national star, Hollywood could no longer fail to spread out a red carpet for him. It was to RKO—in the person of George Schaefer, its president at the time—that the honor fell of dealing with this young and demanding celebrity. His demands, moreover, were not so much financial as legal and artistic. Welles intended to obtain what terrifies Hollywood the most—total freedom. Nor would he agree to part with his Mercury Theatre friends. So the negotiations were painstaking, but Welles finally won his case and was given, in August 1939, a contract unique in the annals of Hollywood. In it was stipulated that he would make one film a year, by choice as a producer, director, scriptwriter or actor, or all at once. He would be guaranteed 25 percent of the gross profits of each film, on which he would receive an advance of $150,000.

These exceptional arrangements had the effect of sharply antagonizing Hollywood toward the "genius" who wanted to upset everything. He was made fun of and, in particular, blackballed; there were few people at the party he had organized to celebrate his arrival. His careless dress and a lush beard, intended to round off his characterization in the film he planned to make, provoked the malice of caricaturists. In short, jealousy did its work!

Welles, who feigned indifference, took refuge with an army of secretaries in a luxurious mansion on top of Brentwood Hill, where he enthusiastically prepared the film adaptation of the work he had chosen: Joseph Conrad's *Heart of Darkness.* It was an adventure drama set in central Africa; Welles was to play the role of Kurtz, whom the narrator of the story, Marlow, tries to save.* Welles' idea, original at the time, was to retain the novel's first-person narrative: thus Marlow, identified with the camera, would never be seen. It's possible, even probable, that the idea came to Welles from his radio programs, in which he was both the personable host and first-person focus. Whatever the case, we know what came of it. It took an Orson Welles to think of it, but it was Robert Montgomery who achieved it some years later in *The Lady in the Lake,* in the most unconvincing manner possible. But perhaps it was also, in any event, a "false" good idea and we shouldn't have too many regrets that Welles had to abandon it.

The preparation of *Heart of Darkness* was almost finished when war broke out, depriving RKO of its European markets, an awkward prospect for a film costing more than a million dollars. Moreover, the star who had been cast and hired, Dita Parlo, was "interned" in France as an Austrian alien. Quite worried, Schaefer abandoned the project and suggested to Welles, as a replacement, a more traditional thriller: *The Smiler with a Knife,* written for fun by the English poet C. Day Lewis.† But this new project failed in turn because the stars approached—Carole Lombard and Rosalind Russell—each refused to take risks with this young and inexperienced eccentric. Our thanks are due them, for it was their caution that brought to the surface a third project, conceived by Welles and Mankiewicz: *Citizen Kane.*

*In a 1972 interview, Welles stated that he initially intended to play only Marlow, and subsequently decided to portray Kurtz as well. Cf. Jonathan Rosenbaum, "The Voice and the Eye," *Film Comment,* November–December 1972. (*Trans.*)
†Under the pseudonym Nicholas Blake. (*Trans.*)

Citizen Kane

Which brings us to the spring of 1940. Houseman, Mankiewicz and Welles worked for over three months on this new screenplay, and finally the production got under way, beginning before the assembled press on July 30, 1940. In *Motion Picture Herald* the next day, an article was headlined: "Silence! Genius at work." It was then exactly one year since Orson Welles had arrived in Hollywood.

That year, contrary to appearances, had certainly not been wasted. Welles' remark when he first visited the RKO studios is well known: "This is the biggest electric train set any boy ever had!" Obviously the remark of a child; but it didn't remain that for long. Welles benefited from those long months of semi-inactivity and delays between the summers of 1939 and 1940 by methodically exploring all of the studio's mechanics and the secrets of filming, and by having numerous films projected for him. So he undoubtedly embarked upon the direction of *Citizen Kane* richer in technical and artistic knowledge, which he wouldn't have possessed if he had had to set to work immediately.

The shooting of *Citizen Kane* lasted fifteen weeks. The film was ready for editing on October 23, 1940. Its filming had been carried out in an atmosphere of great secrecy, and there is a well-known story about an army of producers who, having dared to invade the set while shooting was in progress, found the actors playing baseball under the director's orders. Despite—or perhaps because of—this discretion, rumors were afloat concerning the scandalous nature of the screenplay. The famous columnist Louella Parsons—employed by the newspapers of the press magnate William Randolph Hearst—who up to that time had supported Welles, felt obliged to inform her boss that the fictional biography of the film's hero was said to be largely inspired by the life of Hearst himself. What followed proved that these rumors were not without foundation. Despite formal denials on the part of Welles and RKO, Hearst nevertheless got permission for his lawyers and Miss Parsons to

The Young Kane with his sled, *Citizen Kane,* 1940 (National Film Archive)

Deep focus in the banquet scene, *Citizen Kane* (National Film Archive)

Susan's attempted suicide, *Citizen Kane* (National Film Archive)

view the film when editing was complete. What they saw was sufficiently enlightening and Hearst tried, to all intents and purposes, to forbid the release of the film. In point of fact, the legal case was very weak, and Schaefer, like Welles, knew this perfectly well. They stood firm, and the commercial release of *Citizen Kane* was even announced with wide publicity for February 14, 1941. Hearst, having no illusions about the legal situation, then resorted to a less official but very effective form of artillery. His newspapers boycotted RKO films and initiated a vicious compaign against the company, while the other large Hollywood studios underwent effective pressures. There was even a question at one point of creating a consortium to buy up the negative and destroy it.

Welles, unperturbed, declared during after-dinner speeches that if they continued to rub him the wrong way, he was going to start work on a great idea for a screenplay based on the life of . . . William Randolph Hearst. Things might not have gone so far if the fire hadn't been carefully stirred up by another scandal-sheet columnist, Hedda Hopper, who supported Orson Welles against her rival Louella Parsons, and did so to such an extent that the controversy wound up sowing discord in the very heart of RKO headquarters, where Schaefer had to make sacrifices. The release of *Citizen Kane* was delayed from week to week, and a worried Welles decided to threaten RKO publicly with proceedings on the part of himself and Mercury Theatre for breaking the contract. Fortunately, he didn't have to follow through with this action; for that matter, RKO, which had already spent over $800,000 on the film, was just as anxious to get its money back. Despite Hearst's fury, *Citizen Kane* was therefore presented to the press on April 9, 1941, simultaneously at the Broadway Theatre in New York and the Ambassador in Los Angeles. It was an enormous success, and the next day the critics were deliriously enthusiastic. News of this triumph doubtless contributed to the recovery of Orson Welles, whose doctor, fearing a nervous breakdown, had sent him to rest in a Palm Springs clinic.

Unfortunately, this critical success was to remain a *succès d'estime* which the public was not going to follow. An "adult film," *Citizen*

Kane proved to be decidedly above the mental age of the average American spectator. At the very most, it helped to raise it. In short, despite the scandal and the critical reception, Welles' first film was a very bad financial deal for RKO.

Pending a more detailed analysis, let us restrict ourselves for the moment to recalling the film's subject. Better still, let us leave this task to the director himself:

> *Citizen Kane* is the story of a search by a [journalist] named Thompson . . . for the meaning of Kane's dying words. . . . He decides that a man's dying words ought to explain his life—maybe they do. He never discovers what Kane's mean. But the audience does. His researches take him to five people who knew Kane well—people who liked him or loved him or hated his guts. They tell five different stories, each biased, so that the truth about Kane, like the truth about any man, can only be calculated by the sum of everything that has been said about him.
>
> Kane, we are told, loved only his mother—only his newspaper— only his second wife—only himself. Maybe he loved all of these, or none. It is for the audience to judge. Kane was selfish and selfless, an idealist, a scoundrel, a very big man and a very little one. It depends on who is talking about him. He is never judged with the objectivity of an author, and the point of the picture is not so much the solution of the problem as its presentation.

The only thing one should add, because it does not emerge clearly from this accurate summary, is that these fragmented story lines let Orson Welles play freely with chronology. It was no longer respected. The various testimonies emphasizing one event or another would inevitably overlap, each constituting a return to the past between the returns to the present of the investigating journalist. Since *Citizen Kane,* the procedure known as the flashback hasn't been developed, and it certainly wasn't original in 1941, but up to that time it had been employed only rarely, and generally without chronological superimposition (cf., for instance, *Le Jour Se Lève,* made a short time before the conception of *Citizen Kane*). Afterward, moreover, the return to the past has been used most often only in a much more elementary way, as a narrative convenience, while in *Citizen Kane,* as we shall see, it is raised to the dignity of a metaphysical viewpoint. In any case, if Welles did not actually invent the flashback, his film introduced it into the current cinematic language. The history of scriptwriting was incontestably turned topsy-turvy by it. As for the history of direction, we shall see that it wasn't left behind.

An amusing detail: while today the Academy Awards readily dispense quintuple Oscars to pretentious pseudo-intellectual enterprises, they could find only one to give to the author, actor and director of *Citizen Kane:* for best screenplay.

Orson Welles returned to Hollywood at the end of 1941 to fulfill his contract to make three more films. In theory, the program should have been all mapped out, but after the drama of *Citizen Kane* and the public's resistance, Welles' authority was more than a little shaken, as was perhaps the confidence of Schaefer. In short, there was no longer any question of the audacities of *Heart of Darkness,* nor even of *The Smiler with a Knife.* * At one point, *The Pickwick Papers* was mentioned, but they finally fell back on a less problematical novel, by Booth Tarkington: *The Magnificent Ambersons.*

The Magnificent Ambersons

Less famous, because it wasn't surrounded by an aura of scandal, and also because Welles chose not to appear in it as an actor, *The Magnificent Ambersons* is probably no less important than *Citizen Kane;* it is even possible to prefer it. This in fact is the opinion of Orson Welles, whom I have heard contrast the unity and simplicity of *Ambersons'* style to the "bric-a-brac" of *Citizen Kane.* What one can say is that, reversing the usual process, Welles had produced his "baroque" film before his classical work. Basically, however, what is essential in the stylistic inventions of the first recurs with greater mastery and is more intelligently pared down in the sec-

---

*In theory, *The Smiler* was only put off *sine die,* and Welles had proposed and had RKO accept the idea of making *Heart of Darkness* afterward by forfeiting all the profits that might come from this film.

Orson Welles

Welles with George Coulouris, *Citizen Kane*

Finding "Rosebud," *Citizen Kane*

ond, often pushed even further. Even what struck the critics most forcibly, the social impact of the subject, turns up again, with perhaps more subtlety and depth in this evocation, at once realistic and critical, of America at the end of the nineteenth century and the beginning of the twentieth.

It is the story of a rich family in a small Southern town* whose social supremacy is gradually being compromised by the promotion of industries from Europe and the North. George Amberson Minafer is the arrogant offspring of this line; Isabel, his mother, had formerly been engaged to a certain Eugene Morgan, whom she had rebuffed one day when he made a fool of himself before her. Twenty years later, a widower, Morgan returns with his daughter, Lucy. He has become a prosperous industrialist, having made his name in the automobile business. His fortunes continue to grow while the Ambersons' crumble away. Soon Isabel's widowhood will legitimize the amorous friendship of Eugene, whom in reality she had never ceased to love. They could now realize their old dream of happiness after twenty years' delay if George's pride, and perhaps some Oedipal feeling, didn't present an obstacle. George, however, is in love with Lucy and clumsily courts her, but this alliance between the traditional pride of the South and the industrial *nouveaux riches,* which wouldn't shock him in Lucy's case, seems like a fall from grace and a defilement in the case of his mother. So he busies himself thwarting her with the complicity of his aunt Fanny, an old maid hopelessly in love with Eugene. Without realizing what he is doing, George brings misfortune on everyone—Morgan, his mother, his aunt Fanny, and himself, for his arrogance discourages Lucy. As the supreme humiliation, after Isabel's death George is forced to earn his living—the landed property of the Ambersons, swallowed up by the factory district, having lost almost all its value. A relatively happy ending, for which Welles is probably not responsible,† arrives *in extremis* to mitigate the sadness of this fate: returning from work, George is knocked

*Tarkington and Welles both identify it as a "mid-land town," indicating that its location can more plausibly be viewed as Midwestern. *(Trans.)*

†Cf. Joseph McBride's *Orson Welles* for a detailed account of the changes. *(Trans.)*

down by a car and taken to the hospital, where Lucy, moved by his misfortune, is reconciled with him.

To be sure, the love intrigues which assume a large place in *The Magnificent Ambersons* are rather conventional. They belong to the family of *Back Street* or *Love Affair/An Affair to Remember;* but the psychological detail and above all the social description renew its meaning and confer upon it an intellectual and moral perspective which completely justifies it.

It was probably this psychological accuracy that caused the commercial failure of *Ambersons,* whose classicism, seemingly more conventional, left the public even more indifferent than had the audacities of *Citizen Kane.* The oracles of RKO did not fail to predict this outcome, and dispensed with Orson Welles when it came to the editing of his film. New transitional shots were probably filmed to alter the story. Some of these, moreover, are easy to spot. And in the bargain, the final editing was done while Welles was in South America, shooting *It's All True.*

The Magnificent Ambersons was performed by Dolores Costello— the widow of John Barrymore, who had scarcely appeared in a film since the silent days—in the role of Isabel; Joseph Cotten, in the part of Eugene Morgan; Agnes Moorehead gave a dazzling portrayal of Aunt Fanny; Ray Collins was Uncle Jack and Richard Bennett played Major Amberson. Anne Baxter was a marvelous Lucy Morgan, with a smile that was at once sorrowful and subtly fixed. As for George, he was played by Tim Holt, whose name had heretofore scarcely been known except in the credits of "B" Westerns. Here he was obviously a stand-in for Orson Welles, with whom he shared a certain physical resemblance. It is saying a good deal that this weighty reference didn't crush him, so strongly had the director been able to instill him with his own personality.

The Great Diptych:
Geology and Relief

The Obsession with Childhood

Before continuing the artistic biography of Orson Welles, this would seem a suitable moment to pause over his work and reflect on its critical significance. There is little doubt that even if he had directed only *Citizen Kane* and *The Magnificent Ambersons,* Welles would have a major position in the history of the cinema. It is not to diminish the importance of his later films if I assert that, at least on a formal level, the essence of what Welles brought to the cinema is already present in his first two films.

Analysis and reflection reveal, above all, a stylistic unity. Within the context of Welles' filmography, these two works constitute a vast aesthetic land mass whose geology and relief justify simultaneous study.

Let us take up their orientation first. *Kane* and *Ambersons* together form what might be called the social realist cycle, to distinguish it both from the Shakespearean cycle composed by *Macbeth* and *Othello* and from the "ethical entertainments" comprising *The Lady from Shanghai* and *Mr. Arkadin.* "Entertainment" should not be understood here in a pejorative or even a restrictive sense. But it is obvious that these two latter films imposed an overall sense of amused contrivance on their thriller conventions. In other words, the seriousness of the message filters through the apparent futility of the game.

Kane and *Ambersons,* on the other hand, are the cinematic equivalents of realistic novels in the tradition of, say, Balzac. On one level they appear to be powerful, critical testimonies on American society.

But one must pass beyond this first level of significance, where one soon reaches, beneath these social deposits, the crystalline mass of moral significance. From this point of view, Welles' *oeuvre* is one of the least debatable in the history of the cinema, and takes its place beside the great spiritual landscapes created by Stroheim, Chaplin, Eisenstein, Renoir, Flaherty, Rossellini. Rather than pursue an exhaustive description and analysis of this message, we shall try to isolate one of the major themes of Welles' imagination as it is revealed in a very special way in his first two films: the obsession with or, if one prefers, nostalgia for childhood. Kane's lust for social power and George Minafer's pride are deeply rooted in their childhoods—that is, in Welles' childhood. We have seen, however, that it was a happy childhood *par excellence,* but nonetheless one that was possibly—and paradoxically—incomplete by virtue of its very happiness. Too many good fairies hovered over his cradle, not leaving the child time enough to live his childhood. So it is not surprising that *Citizen Kane* and *The Magnificent Ambersons* could finally be a matter of a childhood tragedy. The last wish of Kane, the superman, the supercitizen who squanders his fabulous wealth playing with and against public opinion, his "fundamental project," as the existentialists would say, is completely contained in a glass ball where a few artificial snowflakes fall at will on a little house. This grizzled old man, whom no one dares to admit is senile, who almost held in his hand the destiny of a nation, grasps this childish souvenir before dying, this toy that was spared during his destruction of the doll's room belonging to his wife Susan. The film ends on the word with which it began; "Rosebud," whose significance in Kane's life the investigation seeks in vain, is nothing but the word written on the surface of a child's sled. When pride and the alibis of success have loosened their grip, when this old man, on the threshold of death, forgets himself so far as to let slip the most secret key to his dreams in a last reverie, his legacy to history is only the word of a child. Isn't it with the sled, whose perhaps unconscious memory will haunt him until his death, that he violently strikes, at the very outset of his life, the banker who has come to tear him from his play in the snow and his mother's protection, come to snatch him from his childhood to make him into Kane the citizen? "A great citizen"—Kane indeed becomes this because his fortune condemns him to it; but at least he takes revenge on the frustration of his childhood by playing with his social power as a monstrous sled, allowing himself to be intoxicated by the dizziness of wealth or striking in the face those who dared to question the moral grounds of his acts and his pleasures. Unmasked by his best friend and by the woman he thought he loved the most, Kane admits before dying that there is no profit in gaining the whole world if one has lost one's own childhood.

If one had any doubts, on the evidence of a single film, about the obsession with childhood in Welles' work, *The Magnificent Ambersons* would provide a decisive confirmation. Although the screenplay this time was not original but one based on a novel whose plot was imposed on him from the outset, Welles succeeded in infecting the principal character, played by Tim Holt, with the same obsession as Kane. Not that George Minafer is in any way a duplicate of Kane. The social context, the historical moment, the biographical conditions in which the Amberson heir evolves, give his personal drama a completely different character. But his tyrannical attachment to his mother and his opposition to Eugene Morgan—the industrialist who loves her and who represents both economic and social change—form a similar egotistic "fixation" on the universe of his childhood, where he was king (the scene where the young George, dressed in a curious Louis XIV outfit, refuses to apologize is highly significant).

But even more strongly than this superficial reading of the scripts' underlying meaning suggests, the profound authenticity of the theme of childhood in *Citizen Kane* and *The Magnificent Ambersons* is revealed more persuasively by the introduction in the story or *mise en scène* of significant and visibly unpremeditated details, which have imposed themselves on the author's imagination by their affective power alone. For instance, the repeated use of snow, characteristic of childhood fantasies (the snowballs of *Les Enfants Terribles*). Nostalgia for snow is connected to our earliest games (to which should doubtless be added the specific symbolism of snow, whose threatened whiteness, auguring the mire to come, is particularly suited to the guilty innocence of childhood). In *Ambersons,* a fall in the snow becomes the pretext for the first lovers' kiss between George and Lucy. Another detail, this time from the dialogue: the affair between Kane and Susan dates from a meeting when Kane was going alone on foot to a warehouse on the edge of the city to look at some things that belonged to his mother. Indirectly linked to the theme of childhood by way of egotism and the need for social approval is Kane's taste for statues, through which he is obviously pursuing the impossible project of becoming a statue himself.

Once again, this interpretation, which we might call existential, does not pretend in any way to exhaust the meanings of Welles' first two films, whose labyrinths could be traced by other threads. What matters is that one should be no less sure of meeting the Minotaur there. Welles' *oeuvre* is a haunted one—that is all that it was necessary to demonstrate.

The Intuition of the Sequence Shot

But more than the intellectual and moral message—which will become more precise and perhaps richer later on, in the subsequent films—it is their formal brilliance, their overwhelming originality of expression, to which *Citizen Kane* and *The Magnificent Ambersons* owe their historical importance and the decisive influence they have had on cinema all over the world. We can analyze the technique of the *mise en scène* in either film, for despite considerable variations between their styles, the essential aspects of their means of expression are the same. This likeness is all the more revealing in that the technical crew, and the cameraman in particular, are different. Certainly one must not underestimate the merits of Gregg Toland, who, before and after his collaboration with Welles, has shown himself to be a cameraman of genius, to whom the tyro director undoubtedly owed a great deal; but the refined and somewhat sophisticated elegance of Stanley Cortez's photography is at opposite poles to the rugged frankness of Toland's. Nevertheless, the construction of *The Magnificent Ambersons* is founded on the same principles as *Citizen Kane,* principles which therefore certainly originated with Welles. When one has seen and absorbed *Citizen Kane* and meditated, however briefly but without prejudice, on its *mise en scène,* the accusations of plagiarism or of gratuitous eccentricities designed to *épater le bourgeois* soon appear absurd. There are so many inescapable connections between the formal approaches adopted and the film's significance that a desire to astonish and attract attention appears infinitely less probable than a need to recreate a language capable of expressing new realities on the screen. Let us try to reconstruct one of these logical progressions from intention to form.

It is plausible, for example, to suppose that Welles, as a man of the theatre, constructs his *mise en scène* on the basis of the actor. One may imagine that the intuition of the sequence shot, this new unit in film semantics and syntax, grew out of the vision of a director accustomed to placing the actor within the décor, who experienced traditional editing no longer as a fluency or language but as a loss of efficacy, a mutilation of the spectacular possibilities of the image. For Welles, each scene to be played forms a complete unit in time and space. The acting loses its meaning, is deprived of its dramatic blood like a severed limb, if it ceases to maintain a living and responsive connection with the other characters and the décor. Furthermore, the scene charges itself like an electrical condenser as it progresses and must be kept carefully insulated against all parasitic contacts until a sufficient dramatic voltage has been reached, which produces the spark that all the action has been directed toward. Take, for instance, Welles' favorite scene in

Welles and Stanley Cortez on the kitchen set, *The Magnificent Ambersons,* 1942
(National Film Archive)

Tim Holt and Agnes Moorehead in the kitchen scene, *The Magnificent Ambersons*
(National Film Archive)

The fall in the snow, *The Magnificent Ambersons* (National Film Archive)

The Magnificent Ambersons: the one in the kitchen between Fanny and George and, later, Jack. It lasts almost the length of an entire reel of film. The camera remains immobile from start to finish,* facing Fanny and George; the latter, having just returned from a trip with his mother, has rushed into the kitchen to gorge himself on strawberry shortcake prepared by his aunt. Let us distinguish what one may call "the real action" and "the pretext action" in this scene. The real action is the suppressed anxiety of Aunt Fanny, secretly in love with Eugene Morgan, as she tries with feigned indifference to find out if George and his mother traveled with Eugene. The pretext action—George's childish gluttony—which floods the entire screen, submerging Aunt Fanny's shy but distressed vibrations, is deliberately insignificant. For these two actions there are two dialogues: the real one, made up of a few insidious questions, camouflaged in a certain way by the other, crudely banal, in which Fanny advises George not to eat too fast and asks him whether the cake is sweet enough. Treated in the classic manner, this scene would have been cut into a number of separate shots, in order to enable us to distinguish clearly between the real and the apparent action. The few words that reveal Fanny's feelings would have been underlined by a close-up, which would also have allowed us to appreciate Agnes Moorehead's performance at that precise moment. In short, the dramatic continuity would have been the exact opposite of the weighty objectivity Welles imposes in order to bring us with maximum effect to Fanny's final breakdown, exploding brutally in the midst of this insignificant dialogue. Wasn't it more skillful to ease us gradually into this intolerable tension, created from moment to moment, between the real feelings of the protagonists and their outward behavior? Fanny's pain and jealousy burst out at the end like an awaited storm, but one whose moment of arrival and whose violence one could not exactly predict. The slightest camera movement, or a close-up to cue us in on the scene's evolution, would

---

*To dot the *i*'s and cross the *t*'s somewhat, the shot runs for four minutes and twenty-five seconds and contains two brief pans—one at the beginning and another at the end. (*Trans.*)

have broken this heavy spell which forces us to participate intimately in the action. We shall have occasion, returning to Welles' construction from another point of view, to analyze scenes built up in exactly the same manner. It is obvious that this shot was the only one that allowed the action to be set in such relief. If one wished to play at each moment on the unity of the scene's significance, and construct the action not on a logical analysis of the relations between the characters and their surroundings, but on the physical perception of these relations as dramatic forces, to make us present at their evolution right up to the moment when the entire scene explodes beneath this accumulated pressure, it was essential for the borders of the screen to be able to reveal the scene's totality. This is why Welles asked his cameraman to resolve this difficult problem. In the same way, throughout the wonderful sequence of the ball at the beginning of *Ambersons* (a sequence whose construction, moreover, is very close to that of the chase in *La Règle du Jeu*), several centers of interest are perpetually crossing the screen, compelling us to leap from one to the next, regretfully abandoning each preceding one.*

*In an article about *The Magnificent Ambersons* for *L'Écran Français* (November 19, 1946), Bazin also noted: "Thanks to the depth of field, all of the actors participate in the action and the entire set, including the ceilings, encloses them in its presence. In *Ambersons,* the house's interior architecture seems to be completely and continually on the screen, just as one sees the street in its entire length several times, either directly or through the reflections in the shopwindows. The care taken by Orson Welles not to crack this dramatic crystal led him to break with the usual practice of construction by using static shots of vertiginous duration (that of the kitchen dialogue between Aunt Fanny and George), but it would be a simple matter to show that the extended tracking shots arise from the same concern to follow an event in all its developments. It is not so much camera movements as actors' movements within the décor and the variations of lighting which serve the narrative."

Bazin explored this latter point more fully in *"L'Apport d'Orson Welles,"* an article printed in *Ciné-Club* (May 1948): "Choosing examples from *Kane* and *Ambersons,* it would be easy to demonstrate that the dramatic and technical construction, even though it didn't radically upset basic filmic matters, testified to a singular inventive power that already was in the *mise en scène.* In particular, the frequent use (remarkably subtle and assured in *Ambersons*) of what one could call the counteremphasis of the subject has never been pushed so far. I mean by this the refusal to let the spectator see the climactic events of a scene. This dramatic procedure should in no way be confused with ellipsis, which is cited, perhaps incorrectly, as the basic rhetorical figure of cinema; it should be linked, rather, with litotes [understatement]. With Welles, the entire film is partially pulled out of our reach, and all the action seems to be surrounded by an aura of inaccessibility. In *Ambersons* particularly, the lighting of Cortez, the cameraman, probably serves in one respect to restore the ambiance of gaslight, and in another respect, enables Welles to let the actors evolve in a luminous heterogeneous space, where the alternations of clear and shadowy areas restore, within the

The Technique of Wide Angles

But the clarity of the scene in depth was not enough for Welles'
theatrical approach; he also needed a "lateral" depth of focus.
This is why Gregg Toland used very wide-angle lenses, bringing
the angle of the shot close to that of the eye's normal vision. These
wide-angle shots are perhaps even more characteristic of the style
of *Citizen Kane* than the depth of focus (in *The Best Years of Our Lives*,
Gregg Toland seems mainly to have used "long focal lengths,"
giving a narrow angle and a "telephoto" effect). Initially, it was
because of the exceptional openness of this angle of vision that the
presence of ceilings became indispensable to hide the studio
superstructures. Their installation must have singularly complicated the lighting problems, especially as with very reduced iris
stops a strong light was necessary, which was the origin of the high
contrasts in the images. This must have been counteracted on
several occasions by using false netted ceilings which permitted
light to come across.* Wide-angle lenses also have the effect of
distorting perspective appreciably. They give the impression of a
stretching of length, which accentuates the deep focus even more.
I won't risk the hypothesis that Welles planned this effect; but in
any case he has turned it to his advantage. The stretching of the
image in depth, combined with the nearly constant use of low
angles, produces throughout the film an impression of tension and
conflict, as if the image might be torn apart. No one can deny that

immobility of the sequence shot, a sort of *découpage* and dramatic rhythm. But it will
frequently be noted that Welles takes paradoxical care to have the most important lines
uttered precisely when the actor is least visible. Thus the strong moments in the action
escape us at the very instant when our desire to grasp them is most acute. The famous
kitchen scene in *Ambersons* between George and Aunt Fanny can be partially explained in
relation to this. The *refusal* to move the camera throughout the scene's duration, particularly
when Agnes Moorehead has her emotional crisis and rushes away (the camera keeping its
nose obstinately glued to the strawberry shortcake), is tantamount to making us witness the
event in the position of a man helplessly strapped to an armchair." (*Trans.*)
*"None of the sets was rigged for overhead lighting, although occasionally necessary
backlighting was arranged by lifting a small section of the ceiling and using a light through
the opening"—Gregg Toland, "How I Broke the Rules in *Citizen Kane*," *Popular Photography*,
June 1941. (*Trans.*)

there is a convincing affinity between this physical aspect of the image and the metaphysical drama of the story. As for the ceilings, expecially in *Ambersons,* they help situate the characters in a closed universe, crushed on all sides by the décor. In a remarkable and indispensable study of space in the cinema,* Maurice Scherer† has demonstrated conclusively the role of the spatial structures of the film image. Indeed, the significance of directions of movement has long been recognized in painting, and everyone now agrees in marveling at the famous vertical distortions in El Greco. Why, then, should what one proclaims to be full of meaning and high aesthetic value in a traditional art instantly cease to be a valid process as soon as it is used in cinema? Why should Orson Welles be nothing but a show-off and a sensation-monger when he imprints the same formal characteristics on all his work? Certainly Orson Welles is neither the inventor of low angles nor the first to use ceilings, but when he wanted to play with technique and astonish us with a dazzling formal display, he made *The Lady From Shanghai.* The persistence of the low angle in *Citizen Kane* means, on the contrary, that we quickly cease to have a clear awareness of technique even while we continue to submit to its mastery. Thus it is much more likely that the method corresponds to a precise aesthetic intention: to impose a particular vision of drama on us—a vision that could be called infernal, since the gaze upward seems to come out of the earth, while the ceilings, forbidding any escape within the décor, complete the fatality of this curse. Kane's lust for power crushes us, but is itself crushed by the décor. Through the camera, we are capable in a way of perceiving Kane's failure at the same time we experience his power.

Construction in Depth

Up to this point I have been attempting to account for the choice of technique employed by Welles on the basis of his creative psy-

*La Revue du Cinéma, No. 14.
†A pseudonym used by Eric Rohmer. (Trans.)

chology, in relation to his past and his tastes. But let us abandon this subjective point of view, at the risk of limiting the scope of our analysis. Whatever Welles' intentions were, conscious or not, his films remain, independently of what we know about their author. The influence of *Citizen Kane* on the evolution of cinema—its importance as a model—goes far beyond the admirable lesson in dramatic direction which I have tried to analyze. Beyond the new way of developing a particular scene, it was the very structures of film language—such as they were almost universally practiced around 1940, and in most cases still are today—that Welles came along to upset.

I shall deliberately not dwell on the narrative originality of *Citizen Kane,* on the decomposition of time and the multiplicity of points of view. Welles is not really the inventor of this in the cinema, and the procedure was obviously taken from novels. But he perfected its use and adapted it to the resources of cinema with a comprehensiveness that had never yet been achieved.

But I shall pass lightly over these aspects of Welles' films, since they offer no difficulty for even the uninitiated spectator, provided he shows a little good faith. A bit of attention and reflection is sufficient.

In short, it would be better to spend some time on more specific innovations, where a certain familiarity with film analysis is perhaps necessary if one is to be able to distinguish them from the unity of the *oeuvre.* We shall see, moreover, that they are directly dependent on the subjects and their treatment.

We have seen that the value of deep focus, so passionately contested by some, probably lay for Welles in a certain way of placing the décor and characters. But it involves many consequences in addition to the construction of ceilings and a denser style of acting. To begin with, its technical demands make shot transitions more difficult. In any case, Welles was not the sort of man to stop at such a difficulty, even though the decision to have the whole scene played in the camera's distinct field of vision was contradictory to the classical practice of shot transitions. Better still, Welles quite often reinforces the maintenance of this dramatic unity by refusing to use camera movements that would in fact reestablish, by the succession of new framings, a hypothetical breakdown into shots. But we must perhaps recall here, for greater clarity, what we mean by breakdown into shots.*

Whatever the film, its aim is to give us the illusion of being present at real events unfolding before us as in everyday reality. But this illusion involves a fundamental deceit, for reality exists in a continuous space, and the screen in fact presents us with a succession of tiny fragments called "shots," whose choice, order and length constitute precisely what we call the film's *découpage*. If, through a deliberate effort of attention, we try to see the ruptures imposed by the camera on the continuous unfolding of the event represented, and try to understand clearly why we normally take no notice of them, we realize that we tolerate them because they nevertheless allow an impression to remain of continuous and homogeneous reality. In reality we don't see everything at once either. Action, passion or fear makes us proceed to an unconscious *découpage* of the space surrounding us. Our legs and neck didn't wait for the cinema to invent the tracking shot and the pan, nor our attention to contrive the close-up. This universal psychological experience is enough to make us forget the material lack of verisimilitude of *découpage,* and enables the spectator to participate in it just as he does in a natural relationship with reality.

In contrast, let us examine a typical Welles scene: Susan's attempted suicide in *Citizen Kane.* The screen opens on Susan's bedroom seen from behind the night table. In close-up, wedged against the camera, is an enormous glass, taking up almost a quarter of the image, along with a little spoon and an open medicine bottle. The glass almost entirely conceals Susan's bed, enclosed in a shadowy zone from which only a faint sound of labored breathing escapes, like that of a drugged sleeper. The bedroom is empty; far away in the background of this private desert is the door, rendered

*Bazin's term here is *découpage,* a word translated variously as "construction," "cutting" or "breakdown into shots," depending on the context. For a detailed account of the separate meanings and uses of this word, cf. the first chapter of Nöel Burch's *Theory of Film Practice* (Praeger, 1973). (*Trans.*)

even more distant by the lens' false perspectives, and, *behind* the door, a knocking. Without having seen anything but a glass and heard two noises, on two different sound planes, we have immediately grasped the situation: Susan has locked herself in her room to try to kill herself; Kane is trying to get in. The scene's dramatic structure is basically founded on the distinction between the two sound planes: close up, Susan's breathing, and from behind the door, her husband's knocking. A tension is established between these two poles, which are kept at a distance from each other by the deep focus. Now the knocks become louder; Kane is trying to force the door with his shoulder; he succeeds. We see him appear, tiny, framed in the doorway, and then rush toward us. The spark has been ignited between the two dramatic poles of the image. The scene is over.

To really understand the originality of this *mise en scène*—which may appear natural, so effortlessly does it achieve its goal—one must try to imagine what anyone else but Welles would have done (give or take a detail or two).

The scene would have been split up into at least five or six shots. For instance: a close-up of the glass and the pills, a shot of Susan sweating and breathing heavily on her bed (at this moment, the off-screen sound of the knocking on the door), a shot of Kane knocking on the door, creation of suspense by brief cross-cutting, that is, a series of shots first inside, then outside the room, leading up to a shot of Kane forcing the door open. At that moment, another shot of Kane from behind, rushing toward the bed; and to end, perhaps, a close-up of Kane leaning over Susan.

It is evident that the classical sequence composed of a series of shots, analyzing the action according to the way the director wants us to see it, is resolved here into only one shot. So that Welles' *découpage* in deep focus ultimately tends to absorb the concept of "shots" in a *découpage* unit which might be called the sequence shot.

Naturally, this revolution in the conventions of *découpage* is of interest less in itself than for its implications. To simplify, let us say that this synthetic language is more realistic than traditional ana-

George, Lucy, Eugene and Isabel at the end of the ball, *The Magnificent Ambersons* (National Film Archive)

lytical *découpage*. More realistic and at the same time more intellectual, for in a way it forces the spectator to participate in the meaning of the film by distinguishing the implicit relations, which the
découpage no longer displays on the screen like the pieces of a
dismantled engine. Obliged to exercise his liberty and his intelligence, the spectator perceives the ontological ambivalence of reality directly, in the very structure of its appearances. Reconsidered
from this point of view, a scene like the static shot of the kitchen
in *Ambersons* is particularly significant. It seems that during the
entire sequence, the camera obstinately refuses to come to our
assistance, to guide us in the perception of an action that we feel
is gaining momentum, even though we don't know when or where
it will erupt. Who knows if it may not be just when we are looking
at George that a revealing expression will cross Fanny's face? And
during the whole scene, objects, outrageously irrelevant to the
action yet monstrously present (cakes, food, kitchenware, a coffee-
pot), solicit our attention without a single camera movement con-
spiring to diminish their presence.

Contrary to what one might believe at first, *"découpage in depth"*
is more charged with meaning than analytical *découpage*. It is no less
abstract than the other, but the additional abstraction which it
integrates into the narrative comes precisely from a surplus of
realism. A realism that is in a certain sense ontological, restoring
to the object and the décor their existential density, the weight of
their presence; a dramatic realism which refuses to separate the
actor from the décor, the foreground from the background; a
psychological realism which brings the spectator back to the real
conditions of perception, a perception which is never completely
determined a priori. In opposition to this "realistic" *mise en scène*,
proceeding by "sequence shots" seized by the camera as blocks of
reality, Welles frequently uses an abstract metaphorical or sym-
bolic montage to encapsulate lengthy sections of the plot (the
evolution of the relationship between Kane and his first wife;
Susan's career as a singer). But this very old procedure, which the
silent cinema abused, finds a new meaning here, in precise contrast
to the extreme realism of the scenes in which events are respected

integrally. Instead of a crossbred *découpage,* in which the concrete event is partially dissolved into abstraction by shot transitions, we have two essentially different narrative modalities. One can see this quite clearly when, after the series of superimpositions encapsulating three years of torture for Susan and ending on a light going out, the screen thrusts us brutally into the drama of Susan's attempted suicide. Jean-Paul Sartre pointed out very aptly in an article in *L'Écran Français* that this was the equivalent of the frequentative form in English: "For three years he obliged her to sing on all the stages of America. Susan's anxiety would grow, each show would be an ordeal for her, one day she could no longer stand it. . . ."*: Susan's attempted suicide.

A Style That Creates Meaning

All great cinematic works doubtless reflect, more or less explicitly, the moral vision, the spiritual tendencies of their author. Sartre wrote in reference to Faulkner and Dos Passos that every novelistic technique necessarily relates back to a metaphysics. If there *was* a metaphysics, the old form of *découpage* couldn't contribute to its expression: the world of Ford and Capra can be defined on the basis of their scripts, their themes, the dramatic effects they have sought, the choice of scenes. It is not to be found in the *découpage* as such. With Orson Welles, on the contrary, the *découpage* in depth becomes a technique which constitutes the meaning of the story. It isn't merely a way of placing the camera, sets and actors [*mettre en scène*]; it places the very nature of the story in question. With this technique, the cinema strays a little further from the theatre, becomes less a spectacle than a narrative.

Indeed, as in the novel, it isn't only the dialogue, the descriptive clarity, the behavior of the characters, but the style imparted to the language which creates meaning.

Far from being—as some persist in saying, assuming inattentive-

*The third and fourth verbs have been adapted here to English frequentative forms to suit the context. (*Trans.*)

ness in the spectator—a return to the "static shot" employed in the early days of cinema by Méliès, Zecca and Feuillade, or else some rediscovery of filmed theatre, Welles' sequence shot is a decisive stage in the evolution of film language, which after having passed through the montage of the silent period and the *découpage* of the talkies, is now tending to revert to the static shot, but by a dialectical progress which incorporates all the discoveries of *découpage* into the realism of the sequence shot. Of course, Welles is not the only promoter of this evolution, to which Wyler's work also gives testimony. Renoir, for example, in all his French productions, did not cease to work in the same direction. But Welles has brought to it a powerful and original contribution which, like it or not, has shaken the edifices of cinematic tradition.

Hollywood 1941–1944:
A Costly Genius

Samba and Melodrama

After *Ambersons,* which he directed without appearing in the cast, Welles played a small role in a film he didn't direct: *Journey into Fear,* based on a thriller by Eric Ambler. *Journey into Fear* turned out to be a rather humorous and fantastic spy story set in Turkey during the war. "Joseph Cotten, in possession of a vital secret, tries to leave the country in spite of the killer assigned by enemy intelligence. He is aided in this enterprise by a big-hearted nightclub singer (Dolores Del Rio)." Orson Welles played the part of Colonel Haki, chief of the Turkish secret police.

In theory, Norman Foster was the director of this film, with Welles producing and acting. In point of fact, it is clear that *Journey into Fear* is to a great extent the work of Welles, who has left his mark on the script, while numerous directorial touches bear his stamp, notably the killer's musical motif, in which one recognizes Welles' taste for musical effects and aural atmosphere. Moreover, after the first press show, dissatisfied with the film's last sequence, Welles demanded and obtained permission to reshoot it.

But in spite of its not negligible charms, *Journey into Fear* clearly

Welles, *Journey Into Fear,* 1942 (National Film Archive)

Joseph Cotten and Dolores Del Rio, *Journey Into Fear* (National Film Archive)

isn't anything more than a light-hearted variation on an ultra-commercial theme. Welles' third film was a far cry from the ambitions of *Heart of Darkness*. The *Daily Express* could write: "Orson Welles, Hollywood's fiery rebel and scorner of film conventions, has come off his high horse and made a brilliant spy thriller."

The fourth project destined to complete the contract between Welles and RKO was of a very different sort. Welles, always interested in political problems, had for a long time been preoccupied with the relations between the U.S. and Latin America, relations that the war made all the more important. He was able to persuade the Co-ordinator of Inter-American Affairs to finance a major film of indirect propaganda on Latin America. Washington guaranteed $300.* On the strength of this subsidy, Welles got RKO to agree to embark on this special enterprise. *It's All True* was to comprise three stories with a documentary basis. The first was to deal with the carnival of Rio and the origins of the samba. The second, *Jangadieros*, told the story of four Brazilian fishermen who became national heroes; the last, *My Friend Benito*, based on a Flaherty script, took place in Mexico in a bullfighting milieu.

The story of *It's All True* rather unhappily evokes that of *Que Viva Mexico!* Welles spent four months traveling around Mexico, Argentina and Brazil. The carnival in Rio excited him so much that he shot some 120,000 meters of color film for the samba episode, naturally going over his budget.

Unfortunately, during this period RKO underwent a palace revolution in which Schaefer, Orson Welles' protector, was the victim. The new front office reckoned that the company had lost enough money with its resident genius and, as often happens, preferred to cut its losses by stopping the new film in midcourse. The 120,000 meters of film reverted to the RKO vaults, never to emerge, and the $600,000 already tied up in the venture was completely and irrevocably lost, since the government subsidy was to be paid only after viewing the completed film. One can only hope that an astute patron or some eloquent archivist may one day succeed in bringing

---

*The correct sum is $300,000. *(Trans.)*

to light the rushes of the only unseen film of Orson Welles, as was finally done with the negative of *Que Viva Mexico!*

All at once the break with RKO, foreseeable for quite some time, was an accomplished fact. Yet for all that, Welles was not discredited as an actor, and offers came to him from various quarters. He accepted that of his friend Houseman, now a producer, to play the role of Rochester in *Jane Eyre,* adapted by Aldous Huxley and directed by Robert Stevenson. Welles had already played Rochester on the radio and had even formerly thought of bringing this somber romantic drama to the screen.

But under the labored and insipid direction of Stevenson, all he was to get out of it was a bigger reputation as an actor, the pleasure of appearing with a false nose, and the ability to pay off some of his back taxes. Although it has been claimed that the actor often directed his director, *Jane Eyre* appears much less Wellesian than *Journey into Fear,* for instance, or even *The Stranger.*

Meanwhile, Welles was not idle. Politics occupied him in many ways during that period. Paradoxically disqualified from the service because of his asthma, this flat-footed colossus threw himself into propagandizing for the Roosevelt administration and entertaining the troops. With the Mercury Theatre, now become the Mercury Wonder Show, he put on a circus in a tent, with his conjuring act as the show-stopper. This act, where one saw Welles cut Marlene Dietrich in half, was included in the film *Follow the Boys* shortly afterward.

In the meantime, Welles worked for Roosevelt's presidential campaign; he even for a time wrote a political column for the *Post* and went on tour lecturing on the dangers of fascism in Europe.

But the year 1944 saw his return to Hollywood for a film which contributed—it must be said—only moderately to his glory. *Tomorrow Is Forever* is a sentimental patriotic melodrama in which we see a soldier reported missing during World War I returning at the beginning of World War II. He had stayed behind in Austria after being disfigured by horrible wounds, but is eventually made presentable again by plastic surgery; he finds himself, by chance, as it were, in the neighborhood of his remarried wife and his son, but

Welles on the set of *The Stranger*, 1946 (National Film Archive)

Loretta Young and Welles, *The Stranger*

Welles, *The Stranger* (National Film Archive)

doesn't want to disturb their happiness. They would have wound up learning his secret but he conveniently dies, taking it to the grave with him.

This perverse melodrama, directed by Irving Pichel, and somewhat redeemed by the performance of Claudette Colbert, nevertheless had a much greater success than *The Magnificent Ambersons* in America and England, and, along with *Jane Eyre*, helped to make Welles a big commercial star.

The producer William Goetz, assisted this time by Sam Spiegel, was a little more inspired in his second film with Welles.* There was a script by Victor Trivas, which John Huston and Anthony Veiller did further work on. It was the story of a Nazi war criminal hiding in a small town in America, where he passes himself off as an inoffensive professor. He even manages to marry sweet Loretta Young, who is disturbed nonetheless by his occasional cruel and cynical outbursts. Edward G. Robinson, FBI agent, trails the suspect, whose essential wickedness winds up betraying him. The film concludes with a very Wellesian showpiece at the top of a clock tower, where a chase has driven the criminal. In the original script, he naturally committed suicide, but as suicide was contrary to the Production Code, a more spectacular if less believable denouement was conceived: Before falling into the void, Welles gets himself hideously impaled on the bronze sword of the automaton that comes out of the old clock twice every hour.

The opportune bowing-out of the director originally slated enabled Orson Welles to direct *The Stranger*, in which one indeed finds again the hand of the supervisor of *Journey into Fear*. This time Welles faithfully adhered to the film's schedule and budget.

If this attempt to toe the line helped to make the style of *The Stranger* a bit more conventional than that of Welles' other films, perhaps it also enabled him to make the most demented work of his career. Indeed, Peter Noble reported that Spiegel, delighted by his collaboration with Welles, completely reassured Harry Cohn, the head of Columbia, who was still hesitant about entrusting Rita

*Actually Goetz's third film with Welles; the first was *Jane Eyre*. (*Trans.*)

Hayworth's husband with the direction of *The Lady from Shanghai*. Spiegel spoke so fulsomely of Welles' methodicalness and economy that the producer put down the phone receiver convinced that he had the model director.

A Film for Rita

The time has doubtless come for a flashback concerning Welles' private life, of which we have scarcely spoken so far except to indicate his marriage to Virginia Nicholson in December 1934. They were divorced five years later, before Welles left for Hollywood; Virginia was subsequently to marry the nephew of William Randolph Hearst's girlfriend Marion Davies. Among the several "fiancées" attributed to Welles in the interim, Dolores Del Rio was for a long time the most serious. But *It's All True* gave the final blow to their breakup and in September 1943, to everyone's surprise, Orson ended up marrying Rita Hayworth, the number one star of Hollywood, whom he had occasionally cut in half during the run of his Wonder Show. This marriage of genius and beauty was to last only four years, though Orson showed himself to be deeply in love with Rita, of whom he was very proud. Reconciliations followed stormy separations until a divorce was decreed in November 1947. Rita naturally retained custody of Rebecca Welles, born in December 1944. It seems that *The Lady from Shanghai* was the result of one of these reconciliations. Rita Hayworth, star of Columbia Pictures, insisted that the direction of her next film be entrusted to her husband. The company heads doubtless believed they were being protected from Welles' caprices by sticking to a thriller of the most conventional sort, by Sherwood King, which Welles adapted into a treatment of only fifteen or so pages. The preparation of the film was accompanied by flashy publicity. Welles gave the world fair warning that he was going to reveal a hitherto unknown Rita Hayworth and, to begin, had her hair cut in front of the press. After which he left for Mexico with the entire crew and lived there for several months while the heads of Columbia remained without news, sometimes for weeks at a stretch. For the sea scenes, Welles paid a fortune to charter Errol Flynn's notorious yacht the *Zaca,* with the celebrated actor himself serving as skipper. They took advantage of the opportunity by gaily cruising in the Gulf of Mexico for seven weeks. On land, operations were no less costly. The native village that Welles chose for shooting certain scenes—before it proved inconvenient to use—was completely rebuilt on another location. It is said, moreover, that the inhabitants, delighted with this change, afterward refused to move back to their ancestral home. In short, the whole region was mobilized for this "low-budgeter" in black and white, which soon cost Columbia as much as a superproduction in Technicolor.

Perhaps Harry Cohn, though disabused about his colleague Spiegel's assurances, might still have been reconciled to these dizzying excesses if the footage he received from Mexico had held out some hopes for a modest commercial success. But the rushes were disheartening. Finally, having completed the film in San Francisco's Chinatown and the interiors in the Columbia studios, Welles turned over the results for the appraisal of the bosses. What they saw flabbergasted them; Harry Cohn found his voice only to offer a thousand dollars to anyone who could explain the plot to him. He didn't have to worry about any takers; Welles admitted later that he would have been incapable of explaining it himself.

The Lady from Shanghai

Lacking a well-constructed plot, *The Lady from Shanghai* nevertheless reveals an action of uncommon—one might even say subterranean—force. The thriller plot serves as little more than a pretext. What counts is the characters and their relationships, and particularly their moral symbolism. In broad terms we can call it the story of an honest man, Irishman Michael O'Hara, hired as a sailor on a millionaire's yacht, and thereby shanghaied, so to speak, into the dark and dreadful criminal ventures to which the beautiful Elsa Bannister, wife of one of the yacht's two passengers, is but a partial stranger. She tries to involve O'Hara in her double game by using her natural charms, and the unhappy young man has great trouble extricating himself from this hornet's nest, after a terrifying chase in a deserted amusement park, where he abandons Elsa in the throes of death.

With *The Lady from Shanghai,* Welles abandoned the experiments and technical innovations of *Kane* and *Ambersons.* Considered strictly from the standpoint of *découpage* and photography, the film is relatively conventional, but the content of the images is hardly that. One could even almost say that *The Lady from Shanghai* is paradoxically the richest in meaning of Welles' films in proportion to the insignificance of the script: the plot no longer interferes with the underlying action, from which the themes blossom out in something close to their pure states. Fundamentally moral themes, which reveal the essential obsessions of Wellesian ethics, and above all, an eminently contemporary awareness of the freedom of choice between good or evil, together with the feeling that this freedom of choice doesn't depend exclusively on the will of man, but is inscribed within a modern form of destiny. The whole film is bounded by two parts of the Irishman's commentary: "When I start out to make a fool of myself, there's little enough can stop me," and the part which accompanies, in the cold light of day, the flight of the hero leaving behind the dying Elsa: "Well—everybody is somebody's fool. The only way to stay out of trouble is to grow old, so I guess I'll concentrate on that. Maybe I'll live so long that I'll forget her. Maybe I'll die trying."

As Jacques Doniol-Valcroze has rightly observed, the average American moviegoer couldn't forgive Welles for killing off Rita. Even worse, he let her die like a bitch on the floor of a hellish chamber while he walked out indifferently, eager to have things over and done with, without even obeying the elementary rule that the heroine should be paid the courtesy of dying in the arms of the rugged sailor. For some years, the misogyny of the American cinema has become a commonplace of intellectual criticism. Rita Hayworth was undoubtedly one of its first victims, and remains, through Welles' genius, its most glorious martyr.

The critics, if not the public, nevertheless gave *The Lady from*

Shanghai a good reception, but the public trailed far behind. This time, the case of Orson Welles was decided. Hollywood had had enough of a genius who in seven years' time had cost it millions of dollars.

Rita Hayworth in *The Lady from Shanghai,* 1947 (National Film Archive)

Welles, *The Lady from Shanghai* (National Film Archive)

Rita Hayworth and Welles, *The Lady from Shanghai*

Around Europe:
Obstinacy and Uncertainty

Orson Welles, who had never in fact lost touch with Broadway, returned to New York. For his theatrical comeback, he persuaded Michael Todd to put on *Around the World in 80 Days* as a musical spectacular. We know that Welles' idea left a strong impression on the producer. Mike Todd balked, however, at the expensive caprices of Welles' staging and abandoned the project, retaining only the rights to the Cole Porter music, which accompanied the film that was produced in 1955. *Around the World* was therefore presented under the auspices of the Mercury Theatre. Receipts were at first quite encouraging, but attendance dropped off before this very expensive venture could make back its costs, and Welles sank all his personal fortune into it.* It was at this point that his troubles with Internal Revenue began—a not unimportant factor in his departure for Europe.

*According to Peter Noble (op. cit.), "a considerable amount of his own money"—by Welles' estimate about $350,000. *(Trans.)*

Macbeth

But before leaving Hollywood, Welles wanted to prove that he could be a disciplined and frugal director in cinema as well as on the stage. He had long claimed that Shakespeare could be filmed very inexpensively, provided that the production was meticulously prepared in advance with extensive rehearsals, and shot more or less in continuity, with the lighting carefully prearranged, once the cast knew their lines and movements. In short, what Welles was in the process of inventing before the fact—which one wasn't in a position to recognize at the time—was the technique of directing for television. Offering at least the attraction of a modest budget, he succeeded in rallying to this project the head of Republic Pictures, which was at that time only a small company specializing in third-rate Westerns. As Welles had promised, *Macbeth* was shot in twenty-one days, but after four months of rehearsals on a converted stage. It cost only $75,000.*

Theoretically the play was performed by the Mercury Theatre group, but in fact it was done by a second company, inferior to the first one, which had meanwhile been dispersed by Hollywood. One can only dream of the Lady Macbeth that Agnes Moorehead would have made! In her absence, Welles gave the part to Jeanette Nolan, a radio actress whose performance was hardly up to standard. Welles himself played Macbeth.

In spite of its uneven casting, *Macbeth* is an extremely arresting work, as much from a Shakespearean and theatrical point of view as from a simply cinematic one. The conscious and pronounced austerity of its budget, its willful theatricality, the laughable barbarism of the costumes, the coarse pasteboard sets and lighting, really shocked the critics, especially as the film was placed in competition at the 1948 Venice Festival against Laurence Olivier's *Hamlet,* made with lavish means according to principles of *découpage*

---

*Peter Noble reports the cost as 75,000 *pounds;* Charles Higham as $800,000; Joseph McBride writes that the film was finished in twenty-three days "for less than $200,000." (*Trans.*)

rigorously opposed to Welles'. Welles felt that prejudice was in favor of the recognized actor of the Shakespearean tradition, and at the last minute withdrew his *Macbeth* from competition.

When it came out in France (not until 1950), the film still divided the critics. It met with scarcely any passionate defenders except among the "young" generation of critics, who were unstinting in their enthusiasm, and in retrospect I think they were right to prefer Welles' *Macbeth*, torn between heaven and hell, to Olivier's Freudian *Hamlet*. Those cardboard sets; those barbarous Scots, dressed in animal skins, brandishing crosslike lances of knotty wood; those strange settings trickling with water, shrouded in mists which obscure a sky in which the existence of stars is inconceivable, literally form a prehistoric universe—not that of our ancestors, the Gauls or the Celts, but a prehistory of the conscience at the birth of time and sin, when sky and earth, water and fire, good and evil, still aren't distinctly separate. Macbeth is at the heart of this equivocal universe, as is his dawning conscience, the very likeness of the mud, mixture of earth and water, in which the spell of the witches has mired him. Thus these sets, ugly though they may be, at least evoke Macbeth's metaphysical drama through the nature of the earthly drama whose metamorphoses they reveal. The psychological ambiguity of Kane is here totally stripped of its biographical connotations. Kane's drama is transposed onto the most elevated plane of ethics and poetry in the case of Macbeth, who wallows in his crimes, but in whom we nevertheless sense a mysterious spark of innocence and something like the possibility of grace and salvation.

The Third Man

Be that as it may, with the shooting of *Macbeth* barely finished, Welles took the film under his arm with the intention of completing the final editing in Rome,* and set out for Europe, where offers

---

*According to Charles Higham, the film remained in California and Welles cabled instructions about the editing from Italy. *(Trans.)*

Welles as Macbeth, 1947 (National Film Archive)

Welles, *Macbeth*

flourished for films which were more often than not potboilers. But Welles had decided to exploit shamelessly his commercial value as an actor with the intention of filming the projects he really cared about and which the American film industry would certainly forbid if the tax collectors didn't. He therefore accepted—for $100,000 and the right to direct his own scenes—the role of Cagliostro alongside Nancy Guild and Valentina Cortese in Gregory Ratoff's film [*Black Magic*], very freely and distantly adapted from Alexandre Dumas.

After this he was Genghis Khan in *The Black Rose* with Cécile Aubry and Tyrone Power, and Cesare Borgia [in *Prince of Foxes*], again with Tyrone Power. Following his stay in Rome and some abortive Parisian projects, Welles appeared chiefly in London, in Herbert Wilcox's *Trent's Last Case, Trouble in the Glen* and *Three Cases of Murder*. In 1954 he returned to France for the part of Benjamin Franklin in [Sacha Guitry's] *Si Versailles M'était Conté*. But the only film that really contributed to his glory as well as his fame was of course the celebrated *Third Man* of Carol Reed, with a script by Graham Greene.*

Irrespective of its cinematic quality, perhaps somewhat overrated, *The Third Man* clearly deserves to be marked as a milestone in Welles' career, not so much for the quality of his performance, which lasts only about ten minutes, as for the astonishing crystallizing process that took place around Welles through the character of Harry Lime. For the first and perhaps only time, this very popular actor finally found the part that would identify him in the public consciousness. All the others had been "character creations," even the role of Kane. It is significant that he played Harry Lime without false hair or makeup. As he appeared in the doorway with his coat collar turned up, he gave the impression of stepping directly out

---

*Bazin's implied chronology here is at odds with those found in other sources. The filmography in Joseph McBride's *Orson Welles*, for instance, lists the following dates: 1947; *Black Magic*; 1948: *Macbeth, Prince of Foxes*; 1949: *The Third Man*; 1950: *The Black Rose*; 1952: *Othello*; 1953: *Trent's Last Case, Si Versailles M'était Conté*; 1954: *Three Cases of Murder*; 1955: *Mr. Arkadin, Trouble in the Glen, Don Quixote*. (*Trans.*)

of his own life. But above all, the topicality of Greene's script equated the ambiguity of his hero with our war-torn world. Personable bandit, in tune with the disillusioned romanticism of the period, archangel of the sewers, an outlaw prowling the zone dividing good from evil, a monster worthy of love, Harry Lime/Welles was, in this case, more than a character: he was a myth. With the exception of *The Third Man,* it is certain that Welles' cinematic activity as an actor since 1947 scarcely deserves to be remembered in the history of cinema. The same happily doesn't apply to his work as a director.

Othello

So many projects have been ascribed to Welles that it's difficult to know which of these he actually conceived and, in particular, which ones he clung to. There are countless anecdotes concerning Welles' fickleness in his ventures, or more precisely, the caprices that followed in the wake of his most enthusiastic projects. Peter Noble recounts an especially cruel one involving Ernest Borneman, the young Canadian who adapted the story of Ulysses for Welles. Above all, one often observes old abandoned projects resurfacing in unexpected forms. If it's probable that Welles thought of bringing to the screen *War and Peace, Julius Caesar, King Lear, Cyrano de Bergerac, Le Portrait d'un Assassin* and the story of Noah, it is certain that he worked on a version of *Moby Dick,* which he had already adapted for the stage, but Huston's film obviously blocked this project. By way of making amends, Huston then offered him the role of Father Mapple, the preacher. Welles gave an unforgettable performance, making one deeply regret that he wasn't cast as Captain Ahab instead of Gregory Peck.

Be that as it may, we must content ourselves with the realized projects, which bear witness to both the obstinacy and the uncertainty of their author, to an extraordinary singleness of mind and an incredible capacity for squandering and indecision. The story

Welles, *Othello,* 1952

Welles, Othello, 1952 (National Film Archive)

of the making of *Othello* and *Mr. Arkadin* would surely constitute a rather astonishing novel.*

Othello was an old project dating back to Hollywood which became crystallized in Venice when Welles decided he would take advantage of his stay in Italy and his earnings as an actor to produce and direct the film in the city of the doges. Although it is difficult to determine just when shooting began on this film, I think one can place it in the summer of 1948. Welles was then "engaged" to Lea Padovani, who was his first Desdemona. But the results of the footage shot that year with an Italian Iago scarcely satisfied Welles, who decided during the winter to change the cast. He then started to audition some English actresses, and summoned his old friend MacLiammoir, from Dublin's Gate Theatre, whom he hadn't seen since 1934, to play Iago. In spite of his astonishment, MacLiammoir wound up agreeing to make his film debut under Welles' direction. A Desdemona, however, still hadn't been found. For a brief time it was Cécile Aubry, but she withdrew during the third day of rehearsals. Anatole Litvak drew attention to Betsy Blair, who had just played in his film *The Snake Pit.* Welles was fired with enthusiasm for this new actress, but then the money ran out. While he went off to make some by doing *The Black Rose,* Welles sent his company away to "rest" in his Roman villa. Although no great art came out of it, *The Black Rose* showed Welles that Morocco was the ideal complement to Venice, and he decided to assemble everyone in Casablanca. They shot in Mogador during the spare time that 20th Century-Fox allowed him away from *Genghis Khan.* Out of the countless anecdotes regarding this epic, at least one is worth repeating. When costumes failed to arrive in time from Rome, it was in theory impossible for Welles to film the scene of Roderigo's murder the next day. To get around this little difficulty, he quite simply contrived to situate the action in a Turkish bath; a few towels were all that was needed!

Welles discovered that Betsy Blair was too modern for Des-

*Cf. Michael MacLiammoir's *Put Money in Thy Purse* (Methuen, 1952), a diary of the making of *Othello,* whose chronology differs somewhat from Bazin's account. *(Trans.)*

demona, however, and Suzanne Cloutier took over the role when the crew returned to Venice at the end of summer, 1949. Then, after a new breakdown in finances, the film was resumed again in winter—thanks to the money Welles got from his backers—in Viterbo, Rome and Perugia. In the spring of 1950 it was necessary to return to Morocco to take care of the matching shots involving Desdemona. At last the filming was virtually finished, but not the film; the editing—and what a complicated affair *that* was—took nearly two years, accomplished in Rome, London and Paris. Finally in 1952, four years after the start of shooting, *Othello* was presented as a Moroccan entry on the closing night of the Cannes Festival, where it shared the Grand Prix with *Two Cents' Worth of Hope.*

Othello is undoubtedly one of the most characteristic and personal of Welles' films; at the same time, from the standpoint of the style adopted, it is the one that is furthest from *Citizen Kane* and even *Macbeth.* The contingencies of the shooting adequately explain this. The extreme fragmentation of the *découpage* is surely not unconnected to the way the film had to be made in fits and starts. It is difficult to imagine the long takes of *Macbeth* under these conditions, and it's likely that the rapid rhythm of the editing elegantly camouflages more than one insoluble matching problem. "Every time you see someone with his back turned or with a hood over his head, you can be sure that it's a stand-in. I had to do everything by cross-cutting because I was never able to get Iago, Desdemona and Roderigo, etc., together at once in front of the camera."

But it would be silly as well as superficial to reduce the technique of *Othello*'s *découpage* to these outside encumbrances. True creators always know how to use accidents in a positive way and fire their imaginations with the fact of material resistance. Out of these practical and unavoidable contingencies, Welles knew how to bring a certain freedom to his style of *mise en scène.*

By Welles' own admission, the recourse to extremely fragmented editing doesn't mean that it represents a set position for him in opposition to long takes, but is merely the result of practical contingencies in the film's realization, particularly the lack of money. *Othello* and later *Arkadin* were broken up into short takes

> because a long take requires a very sizable and skillful technical crew; there are very few European crews capable of bringing off a long take successfully, or technicians who can manage it. . . . in *Touch of Evil,* for instance, I did one shot that took place in three separate rooms, with fourteen actors, where the camera setups went all the way from an insert to long shot, etc., and which lasted a whole reel: it was by far the most expensive thing in the film. So when you remark that I don't do long takes, it's not that I don't like them, it's that I'm not given the means to do them. It's cheaper to do this image and that one and then try to control them later in the cutting room. I obviously prefer to control the elements in front of the camera while it's rolling, but that requires money and the producer's trust.

This declaration is very important because it reveals, firstly, that the long take remains an ideal for Welles, even when he does short takes, and secondly, that whatever the technique of the *découpage,* editing remains for him a creative element of prime importance. From this latter standpoint, *Othello* is a key film, for it is the only one apart from *Citizen Kane* and *Macbeth* in which he controlled the editing.* And Welles assumes full authorship only for those films that he has edited himself in their entirety.

> Editing is essential for the director; it's the only time he has complete control over the form of his film. When I shoot, the sun dictates certain things that I can't fight against, the actor makes certain things happen that I have to adapt to, and the story does this as well; I only concentrate on mastering what I can. The one place where I exercise absolute control is in the editing room; it is only then that the director has the power of a true artist. . . . I search for the precise rhythm between one shot and the next. It's a question of the ear: editing is the moment when the film involves a sense of

---

*According to Bazin's first interview with Welles in *Cahiers du Cinéma,* No. 84 (June 1958), from which most of the quotes in this chapter are taken, the only films in which Welles claimed to have complete control over the final editing were *Citizen Kane, Othello* and *Don Quixote. (Trans.)*

hearing. . . . I work very slowly at the editing table, which always has the effect of incurring the wrath of the producers, who snatch the film from my hands. I don't know why it takes me so long; I could work forever on the editing of a film. What interests me is that the strip of celluloid is performed like a musical score, and this performance is determined by the editing, just as one conductor will interpret a piece of music completely in rubato, another will play it in a very dry and academic way, still another will do it very romantically, and so on. The images themselves aren't enough; they are always very important, but they are only images. The essential thing is the duration of each image, what follows each image; it's the whole eloquence of cinema that one is putting together in an editing room.

Whether the film was shot in long or short takes (a phenomenon essentially dependent upon and relative to the budget of the production), editing is therefore an essential moment in creation for Welles. But it's only natural to suppose that its quantitative—if not qualitative—importance is more apparent in films done in short takes like *Othello,* where the overall tempo is indeed determined at every second by the pacing. It's important to notice and allow for this factor, which comes after the *mise en scène* and is all too often forgotten—all the more so considering that in America it is very rare for directors to control their own editing: the film is taken out of their hands after the shooting and entrusted to another technical crew, who give it its final form. As we know, moreover, this is what happened to *Ambersons, The Lady from Shanghai* and *Touch of Evil.*

Whatever the formal problems may be, *Othello* has also often been criticized for its content. Welles defended himself in these terms:

> In *Othello* I felt that I had to choose between filming the play or continuing my own line of experimentation in adapting Shakespeare quite freely to the cinema form. Without presuming to compare myself to Verdi, I think he gives me my best justification. The opera *Otello* is certainly not *Othello* the play. It certainly could not have been written without Shakespeare, but it is first and foremost

Welles, *Mr. Arkadin (Confidential Report),* 1955

112

Welles with Robert Arden, *Mr. Arkadin (Confidential Report)* (National Film Archive)

an opera. *Othello* the movie, I hope, is first and foremost a motion picture.

It undoubtedly takes a lot of audacity to claim to transpose Shakespeare's text into images in this manner, but as Bertolt Brecht replied to a critic who asked him if he had the right to take liberties with classical texts: "One has the right to do it if one is capable of doing it." I think that Welles proves this in *Othello*.

In any case, as a transposition from stage to cinema, *Othello* provides an aesthetic solution of the greatest interest, and one, for that matter, that is quite the reverse of *Macbeth*'s. One of the main difficulties—if not *the* main difficulty—that have to be overcome in adapting from stage to screen is that of the décor. Most failures of filmed theatre can be ascribed to a lack of appreciation of this problem. The conventions of theatrical action and particularly speech don't accommodate themselves to the realism of cinematic space, which the décor makes concrete. In *Macbeth* Welles chose to recreate a universe that was artificial in every particular, a world closed in on its own incompleteness, like a grotto. In *Othello* the artifice is in the open and recreated from entirely natural materials. Thanks to the swift and jagged editing and the camera angles (which eliminate any possibility of linking up the elements of the décor in the given space, either visually or mentally), Welles has created out of the stones of Venice and Mogador an imaginary dramatic architecture, but one enhanced by all the magic, all the composed and accidental beauties that natural stone alone can have in true architecture, weathered by centuries of wind and sun. Thus *Othello* unfolds in the open, but not at all, however, in nature. Like mirrors, those walls, arches and corridors echo, reflect and multiply the eloquence of the tragic speech.

Return to the Theatre

By bringing us to Shakespeare, the story of *Othello* furnishes us with a natural transition back to Welles' theatrical activity, which he had abandoned over five years before, but which was about to manifest itself anew in an important way, within a European framework, before justifying his return to America. With *Othello* finished or nearly finished, Welles decided to put on a show that he could take on tour to the major cities of Europe. He chose Paris and the Theatre Edouard VII, no doubt counting principally on the Anglo-Saxons who pass through the city or spend some time there during the summer season. The program was composed of a play written by Welles himself: *The Unthinking Lobster,* a fable satirizing Hollywood and its penchant for Biblical films. While making a film about a new Bernadette, Anne de Beaumont—who plays the saint—accomplishes genuine miracles. Suddenly we have the "Zitz-Cosmic" Studio transformed into a place of pilgrimages; the producers go to "devotionals" instead of administrative meetings, etc. Finally the economic disturbances prove to be so serious that the capitalists bitterly resent the intrusion of the supernatural into film production. Thus an executive archangel descends from the clouds to negotiate with the Motion Picture Producers and Distributors Association. There will be no further miracles in Hollywood, but the latter will give up making religious films. One knows, alas, that it was only a dream.

Along with *The Unthinking Lobster,* Welles presented under the title *Time Runs* a very free adaptation of the Faust legend based on works by Dante, Milton and Marlowe, accompanied by a Duke Ellington score. The complete show—comedy and tragedy—went under the general title *The Blessed and the Damned.* In spite of the personal success of Welles and his discovery—the charming mulatto Eartha Kitt, who was taken from Katherine Dunham's ballet company—the Parisian critics praised the staging more than the program. After some time, Welles withdrew his own *Lobster* and substituted a scene from *The Importance of Being Earnest* and another from *Henry VI.* A recital of songs by Eartha Kitt completed the evening.

After Paris, this program was brought to Germany. England should have been next, but the tour finally couldn't be organized, and Welles would have found himself relatively inactive in London if TV hadn't kept him busy for a while. It was during that time that he spoke one evening with Laurence Olivier about how much he'd like to do *Othello* on the stage (perhaps in order to take a rest from doing it on the Movieola). Olivier, who harbored no grudges about the Venice competition, elegantly offered his own hallowed stage, at the St. James' Theatre. Thus the *enfant terrible* from the Madison School wound up triumphantly putting on Shakespeare in the British holy of holies for Elizabethan theatre.

Finally, in autumn 1953, Welles proposed to Peter Brook that they put something on together, and the latter suggested *King Lear*, which he would adapt for American TV. The show was naturally an enormous success. A television company capable of commissioning an adaptation of Shakespeare by two of the greatest directors in the world sounds almost too good to be true.

This success with a very large audience could have served to launch Welles in New York again, if not Hollywood. Indeed, offers were not lacking, but he was then thinking about the subject of a new film that he would make under conditions as independent and as precarious as those of *Othello*—*Mr. Arkadin*—and for the sake of this risk-filled project he turned down advantageous contracts which came from stage, film and TV.

He wouldn't return, as we shall see, until two years later, to direct *King Lear* again, on a Broadway stage. Meanwhile Welles went back to Europe, where, at the same time that he was working on *Arkadin,* he put on his stage adaptation of *Moby Dick* at the Duke of York's Theatre. This astonishing show lasted only a month, but there is a remnant of it that one would dearly like to see: the film version Welles made for English TV. Failing this, let us content ourselves with this little document quoted by Peter Noble, a note on *mise en scène* jotted down by Welles on the stage script of *Moby Dick:*

Wensley Pithey should have, as the actor, a velour hat, preferably green, the very fuzzy type. He wears *pince-nez* with a big broad black ribbon. His overcoat should have a ratty, tatty fur collar, and he should wear spats, which he will later remove. His shirt should be heavy, dark flannel and his trousers extremely serviceable dark material, which he will wear with a broad leather belt with a thick buckle. This costume he underdresses, so that his actor's overcoat covers him. He should have a muffler to hide the absence of a stiff collar.

At the date that I write this short critical biography, there remains, in order to complete our account of Welles' theatrical *oeuvre,* only his return to America at the end of 1955 to stage *King Lear.* The dress rehearsal took place in January 1956 at New York's City Center, a theatre that specialized in classical revivals, but it was marked by technical incidents which only an Orson Welles could have turned to his advantage. The second night, he sprained one ankle, and the third night, he sprained the other one. No longer able to walk across the stage, he played the part in a wheelchair camouflaged as a throne, with one leg in a plaster cast. The results were so convincing, however, that one critic could write: "One wondered if Shakespeare wouldn't have put in a wheelchair for the King if he had one around!"

Mr. Arkadin

Let us now retrace our steps a bit in order to take up the cinematic thread in the labyrinth of Welles' life which was abandoned with *Othello.* This brings us first to *Mr. Arkadin.* Like *Kane,* but more freely in relation to its model, *Mr. Arkadin* is inspired by the personality, if not the life, of one of the great adventurers of the modern world, Basil Zaharoff—the all-powerful arms magnate of humble and mysterious origins who, through operations of a most dubious if not most criminal nature, built, in addition to a prodigious fortune, a façade of respectability that was eventually crowned by a knighthood.

Arkadin is at the height of enormous power. But he has one weak spot: his daughter, raised in a convent, coddled and spoiled, and guarded by an army of detectives from strangers who might make her suspect the truth about her father, his origins and his fortune. One of them, however, succeeds in approaching her and arousing her interest. Arkadin grows worried and finds, he believes, a crafty

117

way of getting rid of this Van Stratten, who is nothing but a petty adventurer himself. His method is audacious and paradoxical. He gives the young man the job of investigating his mysterious past, for, he claims, due to amnesia he has forgotten everything, including his original identity. In fact, something quite different is afoot: Arkadin knows that, scattered in various parts of the world, there remain a few witnesses to his crimes whose very existence threatens his fortune and above all his reputation. This idiot Van Stratten is to be responsible for finding them in the hope of gaining the right to see the millionaire's daughter again. All that Arkadin needs to do is kill the prey each time it has been flushed out of hiding, until eventually he can get rid of the flusher himself. Van Stratten finally understands the threat to himself, however, and is driven in self-defense to strike at Arkadin through the single chink in his armor, by revealing to his daughter who her father is. Arkadin then prefers to disappear from his plane in midflight, as luckless as Empedocles leaping into the volcano.

Although Welles had a Parisian producer this time, Louis Dolivet, the making of *Arkadin* was a long and laborious matter. The shooting itself lasted seven months (three months for the basics, four for the continuity shots) and took place in France, Spain and Germany. But the film, begun in 1954, was ready for release only in 1957, due to the length of time taken by the editing (nearly eight months, and even then not finished by Welles) and, in particular, the post-synchronization (done by the actors themselves), to which Welles attached a very special importance. Even though the difficulties of shooting in relation to the actors' schedules were nothing like those of *Othello,* it is certain that here again they played a decisive part in breaking up the *découpage* with cross-cutting; several important scenes were clearly shot in two sets of takes at very different dates in accordance with the availability of the characters. Under these circumstances, moreover, Welles is capable of demonstrating that he can be the fastest director in the world. All the reverse angles in a sequence as important as Katina Paxinou's were done in a single day; those involving Suzanne Flon in six hours. It is true, though, that simple continuity shots of someone getting out of a car were enough to turn the producer's hair gray.

Even so, and even if the technique of the *découpage* is due to the peculiar circumstances of the shooting, Welles was able to integrate this into the very substance of his film. And he closely combined the effects of editing with those of shooting. In *Citizen Kane* and to a certain extent in *Othello,* Welles had already made extensive use of lenses with a short focal length, violently accentuating perspective and giving very characteristic distortions, especially in low angles, perceptible even in the actors' faces. Starting with *Arkadin,* he would systematically and almost exlusively use the 18.5mm lens, which gives both considerable depth of field and a violent impression of spatial distortion. An actor walking toward the camera appears to be wearing seven-league boots.

As Eric Rohmer has so rightly and so well pointed out:

> On the contrary, never have these distortions and this delirium been . . . so well used and justified. The truth which crumbles in the hands of the investigator, right into mortal dust, the scraps of a past which collapse like a sand castle, could not be met head on, and needed to have both their crushing weight and their flimsiness underlined. Welles makes use of a mechanism that no one else has ever really understood, as though he were its owner and inventor. Already praised, and rightly so, for his use of the static shot, since *The Lady from Shanghai* and particularly in *Othello,* he has preferred to fragment his *découpage* as much as possible without disturbing our modern demand for continuity. It has been observed that his favorite rhetorical device is litotes, with the strong point of the scene remaining in the background in front of an impassive camera. Here he piles angle upon angle, but these flourishes don't add up to a closer approach. The camera seems to suffer from the same malaise as the characters who whirl about, reeling. I'm thinking of the section on the yacht, in rough seas, when the drunken Mily reveals to Arkadin the secrets which will lead to her death. Everything, at every moment, seems to be carried away on the swell of a great tidal wave. Even though it only appears in snatches, the sea roars in an undertone. The likeness between Arkadin and an "earth-shaking god" is not, I wager, fortuitious.

Eric Rohmer also wrote the following, and as I couldn't express it better, I will yield the pen to him:

> This story, then, is not so much incredible as fantastic, all the more fantastic in that it doesn't have any recourse to the staples of modern enchantment, exoticism and science fiction. Even leaving aside the symbolism and considering only the plot, it is an absolutely brilliant illustration of a genre which has become more and more debased—when it has not become hopelessly overintellectualized—since Jules Verne and the Fantomas stories. It creates something which is nearly impossible today, a romantic fiction that involves neither the future nor any removal from one's usual surroundings. In a century in which journalism and memoirs of all kinds have made us more demanding about accuracy of detail, we discover our familiar Europe in a strange light and recognize it nonetheless. This unrealistic tale rings even more true than many narratives where care has been taken to ensure verisimilitude. If Welles neglects many justifications which are ploddingly sought after elsewhere, he doesn't play tricks with the kind of truth whose reconstruction the cinema finds most to its taste. This film, it is said, "looks cheap"; it didn't require costly sets and all the technical aids whose presence can be discerned by specialists. But the uninitiated viewer would find that it is very rich, richer than any European or American film released this year, and he would be right. What is so prodigious about the millionaire Arkadin to the man in the street, which we all are in some fashion? His wealth resides less in possessions than in that most modern of powers, mobility, the ability to be present at practically the same time in every part of the globe. A life of travel, of palaces, seems gilded with a magic that sedentary luxury has lost. Most of the time, Welles made a point of taking his crew to the very location where the action is supposed to take place, and this paid off. The actors, who are all excellent, create "characters" but also play on their own physical and even ethnic qualities. The power of money is depicted with a precision that only Balzac would not have envied. All these real elements make up an exceptional world, which we believe in all the more because it is presented as exceptional.

Who is Arkadin really? One of those adventurer figures our age has given us a few examples of, a Basil Zaharoff, a Serge Rubinstein?

No doubt he is, but he is too far removed from the common mold, and resembles too closely the "god Neptune" not to stand for something more: the personification of destiny, a modern, ubiquitous god, returning to the heavens from which he seems to have come (his death isn't shown to us and the plane crashes quickly), a vulnerable god, a cruel god, but also one who is just. Van Stratten saves his own skin but loses the love of Raina, who upbraids him for having placed his own life over that of her father: he is guilty of a sin that is not so much moral as metaphysical. . . .

The case of Orson Welles recalls in many instances that of Stroheim. But I prefer, rather, to compare the author of *Citizen Kane* to Eisenstein. Both have the same set purpose, which, admittedly, is more didactic in the latter's case; both have the same skill in using the camera's *foremost* power, to transfigure reality on the plane of shooting; both have the same confidence in the effects inherent in real or theoretical *montage,* carrying grace to the implicit or explicit "attraction"* (as opposed to Hitchcock, whose recourse to ellipsis and camera movements is a function of *découpage*), the same talent for expressing not only the feeling but the *idea.* We must place them among the greats, even if we refuse to let ourselves be hypnotized by their brilliant example.†

*A reference to Eisenstein's "montage of attractions," a concept developed in his first published article. Cf. the excerpt published in *The Film Sense* (Meridian Books, 1957). (*Trans.*)
†*Les Cahiers du Cinéma,* No. 61 (July 1956).

Return to Hollywood: "Using Up My Energy"

─────✧─────

After *Arkadin,* Orson Welles' filmography finally brings us back to Hollywood. It took nearly ten years for the movie capital to forgive its prodigal son—cautiously, and not without certain reservations —and call him back to the fold. Between 1956 and 1958, Welles played two acting parts and then made a film as both actor and director.

There is unfortunately little to be said about the two acting parts. The first was in a very mediocre "B" film, *The Man in the Shadow,* produced by Zugsmith for Universal, in which he plays the part of a wicked ranch owner who won't tolerate a new sheriff attempting to limit the tyrannical authority he holds over the region. The second was in a more lavish and respectable production, Martin Ritt's *The Long Hot Summer,* based on a short story by Faulkner. Here he gives a thundering performance as the rich, possessive father. This polished and clamorous characterization is interesting only because it shows us the new face and figure of Welles in his early forties. He is more Shakespearean than ever, but nothing remains of the charming romantic hero: he is monumental, enormous, and—according to one's moral lights—olympian or monstrous.

This new personality undoubtedly derived from the extraordinary character which Welles foisted upon himself in the film which he wrote and directed for Universal in 1957, *Touch of Evil.*

Touch of Evil

In the circumstances under which Welles returned to Hollywood, there could, unfortunately, be no question of a new *Citizen Kane;* at the very most, one could hope for a new *Lady from Shanghai.* Even so, it appears that we owe *Touch of Evil* solely to a misunderstanding. In the beginning, there was only talk of a part in a film of the same sort as *The Man in the Shadow,* produced, moreover, by the same Albert Zugsmith, but in order to secure the services of Charlton Heston, the production company stressed the presence of Welles in the project. Heston, thinking that Welles was being employed as a director, accepted on this implicit condition. As a result of this misunderstanding, Welles found himself being offered the direction of a minor detective story. He agreed, not because he liked the subject, but because it was the first offer of work he had received since *Mr. Arkadin.* He was to carry out a transformation of this very ordinary thriller that was analagous to the one effected on *The Lady from Shanghai.* This time, however, it was within a more closely supervised and certainly much more limited budget. To take an example closer in time and spirit, *Touch of Evil* could perhaps be compared to *Kiss Me Deadly,* a film in which Robert Aldrich exploded Mickey Spillane's wretched novel from within in much the same way. And in fact Welles' film adopts the same thriller ethos, pushed to an almost intolerable tension, as well as a sexual sadism that his preceding films had not prepared us for. But however much one may admire Aldrich's film, the relation between *Touch of Evil* and *Kiss Me Deadly* is that of the master's work to his disciple's.

In its underlying thematic pattern, *Touch of Evil* can thus be seen as a masterwork of Welles despite its detective-story pretext. The script opposes a corrupt old policeman convinced of a suspect's guilt and an honest young official who tries to overthrow him. With his back against the wall, Quinlan (the policeman) defends himself by mounting a loathsome plot against the wife of Vargas (the official). The latter manages to extricate himself only by recording a conversation between Quinlan and his best friend. The action takes place in a small border town between Mexico and the U.S.

Considered hastily and superficially, this story seems to oppose the good, honest, democratic policeman and the crooked cop who is ready to sacrifice every principle and pull any trick to frame suspects. His professional ignominy is even further exacerbated by a sickening racism which the mixed population gives him the occasion to exercise. But this fundamental Manicheism becomes turned around and inverted if one pays a little more attention to the script and the characters. Quinlan is not really the crooked cop. He doesn't make anything out of his investigations. He is convinced of the guilt of the people he gets convicted on false evidence. Without him, therefore, the guilty would pass for innocent. Against people's rights, against the intelligence and the honest logic of his Mexican colleague, he opposes the "intuition" which for him guarantees the precision of his diagnosis. If he manufactures evidence, it is because he has to in order to send the "guilty" person to the electric chair. Quinlan is physically monstrous, but is he morally monstrous as well? The answer is yes and no. Yes, because he is guilty of committing a crime to defend himself; no, because from a higher moral standpoint, he is, at least in certain respects, above the honest, just, intelligent Vargas, who will always lack that sense of life which I shall call Shakespearean. These exceptional beings should not be judged by ordinary laws. They are both weaker and stronger than others. Weaker: "When I start out to make a fool of myself, there's little enough can stop me," confesses the sailor Michael O'Hara at the start of *The Lady from Shanghai.* But also so much stronger because directly in touch with the true nature of things, or perhaps one should say, with God. In the final analysis, it is this ambiguity which dominates all of Welles' work since *Citizen Kane.* An ambiguity in which aesthetics are nothing but the reverse of morality. For in terms of beauty, isn't this duality that of Beauty and the Beast? We should not be surprised that Welles' two Shakespearean films are in fact two of the tragedies most consistent with this duality theme, nor in particular that his adaptations plead innocence for Macbeth, pity for Othello. It is not so much the grandeur of evil—although the grandeur is there—as the innocence in the sin, fault or crime. Kane, George Minafer, Michael O'Hara, Macbeth, Othello and Arkadin are all in one way or another condemned by our legal system, our intelligence and even our hearts, but we also feel that they elude our judgment and, implicitly, judge it themselves. To this gallery of ambiguous heroes should naturally be added those potential ones, the heroes of films that Welles would have liked to make, first and foremost Captain Ahab in *Moby Dick.* We should not therefore be surprised that Don Quixote was close to his heart, for in that novel the fundamental duality of moral life is physically expressed in two characters, the Knight and Sancho Panza. It is no accident that the character that made Welles most well known as an actor is that of Harry Lime. Although he is on screen for only ten minutes, Welles clearly polarizes the whole moral meaning of *The Third Man* like iron filings around a magnet. Hank Quinlan should also be interpreted in the light of Harry Lime, but I dare not say that the dialectic of good and evil is more complete and more audacious in this film, for Harry Lime's beauty, his archangelical radiance, gives him a halo of almost superhuman stature to start with. Quinlan, however, has nothing going for him. An ex-alcoholic, ugly and obese, who resists the temptations of whiskey by sucking on candy bars, the archangel is now only a poor devil, his grotesque genius bent to the least noble of tasks. This time, Welles gives his hero no chance; he knows that the public will condemn him. Even the evil that he commits is without attraction. He no longer makes a plea on the grounds of his beauty, however; better than innocence,

Welles as Hank Quinlan, *Touch of Evil,* 1957 (National Film Archive)

Joanna Moore and Welles, *Touch of Evil* (National Film Archive)

Welles, *Touch of Evil*

he pleads on the grounds of a secret superiority.* Let us be sure, however, that we discern it, and raise our voices against the execution of this impossible justice.

As for the direction, *Touch of Evil* is surely not the least interesting of Welles' films. Being less restricted by technical contingencies than in *Arkadin*, and finding the lush Hollywood machinery once again at his disposal, he carried the experiments of his previous film further and brought them closer to perfection. This time the wide-angle lens (the 18.5mm) is used with a diabolical cleverness and mastery, its optical qualities are exploited to the maximum in long sequence shots which conjugate the deep-focus effects of *Citizen Kane* with acrobatic camera movements. The direction seems to be conceived on the basis of two fundamental notions, plastic and rhythmic: distortion of space in depth by means of the 18.5mm lens, and velocity. The *découpage* of *Touch of Evil* is truly vertiginous; the velocity of characters who are always in motion within the frame is superimposed on that of the editing,† which is always linked with the movement. One thinks of the horsepower of huge American cars which allow the driver, just by pressing a lever, to make use of a strong acceleration in overtaking

*In the interests of both history and intellectual honesty, I have to say that in the interviews which he gave me shortly after these pages had been written—interviews published in *Les Cahiers du Cinéma* (Nos. 84 and 87)—Orson Welles challenged this interpretation. He maintains that his moral position is unequivocal and he condemns absolutely Quinlan, Arkadin, Harry Lime, Macbeth and Kane, just as he condemns "all the reincarnations of Faust," but he adds that even if his conscience condemns them unconditionally, he cannot help but admire them in his heart for their "human qualities." It is to this humanity that his talent as an actor lends conviction. Hence the possibility of a certain confusion between the actor and the character, between the devil and his advocate. But does this clarification of the author's contradict my interpretation in any essential way? For even if Welles morally condemns his heroes, is what he calls their "human qualities" anything other than genius? One cannot, of course, doubt the moral, social or political verdict of the author regarding Kane, Quinlan or Arkadin, but if the films were merely the expression of this verdict they would be nothing but films with a message or melodramas. It is the tension created between the grandeur of these condemned heroes and the moral option that we must take against and in spite of this grandeur which makes them tragedies.

†By Welles' own admission, it appears that the final cut made by the studio respected the director's, with the exception of two or three continuity shots added after the event. [This is not quite accurate. For a fuller account of the differences between Welles' cut and the release version, cf. Charles Bitsch in *Les Cahiers du Cinéma*, No. 87, or my own account in "In the Picture," *Sight and Sound*, Autumn 1975, as well as Joseph McBride's letter in the Spring 1976 *Sight and Sound*. (Trans.)]

129

another car. French distributors should really have called *Touch of Evil*—and not *Kiss Me Deadly*—*En Quatrième Vitesse* [*At Top Speed*].

Since I have already analyzed *Mr. Arkadin* at some length, I don't need to linger over the direction of *Touch of Evil,* which is, in some sense, the fulfillment of previous experiments in filming and *découpage.* I should simply add that these experiments obviously run counter to the various wide-screen formats which Welles reproaches for restricting the plastic language of cinema.

The Marvelous Frugality of Television

At the time that I complete this critical biofilmography, the most recent work of Welles that I must mention has to do with television. Even if circumstances had not obliged me to do so, I would have wanted to close on this new art, which derives from a sort of synthesis of cinema, journalism, theatre and radio.

Indeed, it so happens that having been abandoned by the cinema, Welles has found in television an opportunity for self-expression that Hollywood denied him. The frugality of television allowed him, using the money he earned as an actor and on TV, to set up a production of *Don Quixote,* which I can speak about only in terms of what Welles himself has told me. It is a modern version of the Cervantes novel. It was shot in Mexico following a principle of complete improvisation inspired by the early cinema. It will run somewhere between seventy-five and ninety minutes. Though produced for TV, this film will, it seems, be shown in movie theatres. Perhaps it is worth quoting Welles directly on the subject of television:*

> I could invent an aesthetic reason why the movie should be made in this manner, say that there are no other ways of making movies, and so on, but the real reason is that it's a shooting method I'd never tried. I knew that certain masterpieces of the silent era had been made this way. I was also sure that this story would be fresher and

*All of the following quotations from Welles are translated from the French. Unfortunately, the original English text is no longer available. (*Trans.*)

more interesting if I really improvised, and it *is,* without a doubt. Obviously one has to have complete confidence in the actors: it's a very special method of work which is impractical for commercial films.

I should add that the author does not act in *Don Quixote,* but appears in it as Orson Welles.

Welles returned to Europe in the spring of 1958 with his third wife, Paola Mori, the actress in *Mr. Arkadin,* whom he married in 1955 and by whom he had a daughter (his third). His most recent work to date, again for TV, is a *Life of Lollobrigida,* * about which, for the moment, we know only that Welles tells us:

> It's a documentary, if you like, but of a very special kind, with Steinberg drawings, lots of stills, conversations, gossip. . . . In fact, it's not really a documentary at all, but an essay, a personal essay. . . . It's in the diary tradition, me talking about a given subject: Lollobrigida, and not what she's like in reality. It's even more personal than a point of view; it really is an essay.

The critical interest in these remarks should escape no one who wishes to understand better Welles' creative processes, and it is important to add the following:

> The frugality of television is a marvelous thing. The great classic film obviously looks bad on the little screen, for television is the enemy of classic cinematic values, but not of cinema itself. It's a marvelous form when the spectator's only a few feet away from the screen, but it isn't a dramatic form, it's a narrative form—so much so that television is the ideal means of expression for a storyteller. . . . On television, you can say ten times as much in one tenth of the time taken in a movie, because you're only addressing two or three people. And above all, you're addressing the ear. For the first time, in television, cinema takes on a real value, finds its real function in the fact that it speaks, for the most important thing is what you say

*This was never completed. *(Trans.)*

and not what you show. So words are no longer the enemies of film: films only helps words, for in fact television is nothing but illustrated radio.

So TV is above all a way to satisfy my predilection for telling stories, like the Arabian storytellers in the marketplace. I adore that, myself; I never tire of hearing stories told, you know, and I make the mistake of believing that everyone has the same enthusiasm! I prefer stories to dramas or plays or novels—that's an important aspect of my tastes. I read "great novels" with extreme difficulty: I like stories.

The Old Tradition of Experimenters

I'm always looking for synthesis: it's a kind of work that excites me, for I must be honest about what I am and I'm only an experimenter. My sole value in my own eyes is that I don't pass edicts, I experiment; experimenting is the only thing that stirs me up. I'm not interested in works of art, you know, or posterity or fame, just in the pleasure of experimentation itself—it's the only domain where I feel I'm really honest and sincere. I don't have any fondness for what I've done; it really has no value in my eyes. I'm deeply cynical about my work and about most of the works that I see in the world, but I'm not cynical about the act of working on a particular piece of material. It's difficult to explain. We who follow the profession of experimenters are the inheritors of an old tradition: some of us have been the greatest artists, but we've never made the muses our mistresses. Leonardo, for instance, considered himself a scientist who painted and not a painter who might have been a scientist. I don't want you to think that I'm comparing myself to Leonardo; I'm just explaining that there's a long line of people who assess their works according to a different scale of values—you might call it moral values. So I'm not in ecstasy before art. I'm in ecstasy before the human function, which means everything that we do with our hands, or senses, and so on. Once our work is completed, it has less importance in my eyes than it does to most aesthetes: it's the act that interests me, not the result, and I'm only compelled by the result when the smell of human sweat or a thought emanates from it.

Now I write and I paint, I look for ways of using up my energy, for I've spent the better part of the last fifteen years looking for money, and if I were a writer or particularly a painter I wouldn't have to do it. I also have a serious problem with my personality as an actor: I have the personality of a successful actor, which encourages critics all over the world to think that it's about time they took me down a peg or two, you know: "It would do him some good to tell him that he's not all that great." But they've been telling me that for twenty-five years! No, I really have spent too many months, too many years looking for work, and I only have one life to live. So, for the time being, I write and I paint. I throw away everything that I do, but maybe in the long run I'll do something good enough to keep: I have to. I can't spend my whole life at festivals or in restaurants begging for money. I'm certain that I can only make good movies if I write the scripts for them: obviously I could make thrillers, but I have no desire to. The only film that I wrote from beginning to end and was able to complete properly was *Citizen Kane,* and too many years have gone by since I was given the chance. Can I afford to wait another fifteen years for someone who's willing to have total confidence in me again? No, I must find a cheaper means of expression . . . like this tape recorder!

If I have dared to end this provisional biography of Welles with these bitter and disenchanted words, this is first of all because I do not feel that they are without hope. And also because their moving sincerity is a contribution to the psychology of cinematic creation. Nearly all the geniuses of the cinema—Griffith, Stroheim, Gance, Eisenstein—could, at some point or other in their careers, have expressed this bitterness of the artist faced with unjust material hardships in the exercise of their art. Of course, being the *bête noire* of producers doesn't make a genius, but the lines I have just quoted surely convince by their disenchanted sincerity of tone, their nobility and their grandeur, and their modest conviction. Nearly ten years ago, I described Orson Welles as "a Renaissance man in twentieth-century America." I confess that I didn't know at the time how right I was, and that the comparison is even more appropriate today. Explicitly, when we hear Welles proclaim that he is more an experimenter than an artist, after the fashion of the great polymath inventors of the quattrocento, but also implicitly, and against his will, when we see him travel across the earth, as they traveled across Europe, begging for patronage, passing from one court to another in quest of that artist's Holy Grail which exists only in the possibility of creating.

Index

136

Index